THE BRONTËS' IRISH BACKGROUND

Also by Edward Chitham

THE BLACK COUNTRY

GHOST IN THE WATER

THE POEMS OF ANNE BRONTË

BRONTË FACTS AND BRONTË PROBLEMS (*with Tom Winnifrith*)

THE BRONTËS' IRISH BACKGROUND

Edward Chitham

St. Martin's Press   New York

© Edward Chitham 1986

All rights reserved. For information, write:
St. Martin's Press, Inc., 175 Fifth Avenue, New York, NY 10010
Printed in Hong Kong
Published in the United Kingdom by The Macmillan Press Ltd.
First published in the United States of America in 1986

ISBN 0-312-10598-3

Library of Congress Cataloging in Publication Data
Chitham, Edward.
The Brontës' Irish background.
Bibliography: p.
Includes index.
1. Brontë family.   2. Authors, English – 19th century –
Biography.   3. Ireland – Biography.   4. Ireland – Genealogy.
5. English literature – 19th century – Irish
influences.   6. Ireland in literature.   I. Title.
PR4168.C554   1985   823'.809 [B]   85-11999
ISBN 0-312-10598-3

Contents

List of Maps	vi
Acknowledgements	vii
Preliminary Note on the Spelling of Irish Words	ix

1	Introduction	1
2	William Wright, Neighbour of the Brontës in Ireland	6
3	An Irish Presbyterian Milieu	10
4	The Brontë Sensation and its Reception	23
5	Origins: the Brontës in the Seventeenth and Eighteenth Centuries	32
6	From the Boyne to Imdel	49
7	Birth and Childhood of Patrick Brontë	64
8	The Young Patrick	77
9	Brontës in Ireland	92
10	Weird Irish Stories	100
11	The Irish Writing of Patrick Brontë	113
12	*Wuthering Heights*	123
13	Lyric Poems and Rebellion in Gondal	134
14	Charlotte's Irish Accent	142

Appendix: Irish Writers in South Ulster/North Leinster in the Eighteenth Century	152
Notes	155
Select Bibliography	163
Index	165

List of Maps

1. Part of north-eastern Ireland — x
2. Brugh na Boinne and its hinterland — 40
3. Mount Pleasant and Dundalk — 54
4. Patrick Brontë's local townlands — 98

Acknowledgements

This book would have taken a great deal longer to write, and would only have been half as satisfactory, if it had not been for the extremely generous help of Mr Alex Flanigan of Belfast. He has been a tireless and methodical honorary research associate, investigating material in the Linen Hall Library, the Public Record Office for Northern Ireland (PRONI), at Glascar and elsewhere. My debt to him in producing this book is immense.

I should like to express my gratitude to the late Dr W. Haughton Crowe of Rostrevor for his patient replies to my letters, and for locating Bangrove for me. Special thanks are due to Mr C. E. F. Trench of Slane, who spent many hours investigating various matters connected with the Boyne valley. Dr W. D. Bailie of Kilmore gave me great help with the Presbyterian background, and I also wish to thank Mr Noel Ross of County Louth Archæological and Historical Society for information concerning Dundalk and Ballymascanlan.

Thanks are due to Miss Muriel Greene and other members of the Irish Brontë Society for various leads in the search, and I gratefully acknowledge help from the following: Janet Smith of Liverpool Record Office; Dr John Carson of the Presbyterian Historical Society; Dónall Ó Lunaigh of the National Library of Ireland; Kathleen Cann of the Bible Society; Elspeth Simpson of Glasgow University Library; W. H. Crawford of Ulster Folk Museum; Dr Nollaig Mac Congáil of University College, Galway; the Revd Edward Simpson of Hartshead; Seán Mac Labhraí of Craigavon; W. R. H. Carson, Chief Librarian at Portadown; J. Canning, Local History Librarian, Portadown; the Principal of the Belfast Royal Academy; the County Records Officer for East Sussex; J. Harris Rea, MBE, of Banbridge; Miss Rosemary ffolliott of Dublin; Hugh Shields of the University of Dublin; D. R. M. Weatherup of Armagh County Museum. All of these responded to my letters with valuable help.

As always, thanks are due to the Brontë Society at Haworth, in particular Mrs Juliet Barker, curator/librarian, who helped in the search for material relating to William Wright. Any writer on the Irish Brontës must owe a great deal to Dr Wright, who features frequently in these pages. It must be said of him, as of Mr Flanigan, that 'without him this book could not have been written'.

Preliminary Note on the Spelling of Irish Words

It took a great deal of time for Irish place names and personal names to reach a standard spelling. The case is easily illustrated by the name Brontë itself. It would have been written 'Ó Pronntaigh' by a scribe familiar with Irish, 'Prunty' by a person trying to represent the 'p' sound accurately, and 'Branty' or 'Brunty' by those who heard the initial as a softer plosive. The spellings 'Imdel' and 'Emdale' both appear in books, but both are essentially Anglicised forms whose spelling is by no means accurate. In the course of time, such forms began to influence the pronunciation.

I have tried to use the forms of place names printed on the first edition Ordnance Survey under the influence of the Irish-speaking John O'Donovan, who spent enormous effort in seeking out accurate versions of the names. Personal names are rather harder to standardise. I have used the form Eilís for Patrick Brontë's mother. She appears to have written her name 'Allie' at a later stage, but this was probably not short for Eleanor. But Patrick's sister, in the next generation, was called Alice, and it would be futile archaism to try to Hibernicise her name.

After the spelling change to Bronté or Brontë was made by Patrick, the whole family in Ireland adopted this spelling. But their parents, Hugh and Eilís, are more likely to have been written 'Prunty', the form used in Dundalk parish register for another Hugh, who may possibly have been related, or 'Brunty'. Thus in my text 'Hugh Brunty' means the elder Hugh, Patrick's father, who was reared on the banks of the Boyne, and 'Hugh Brontë' means Patrick's brother.

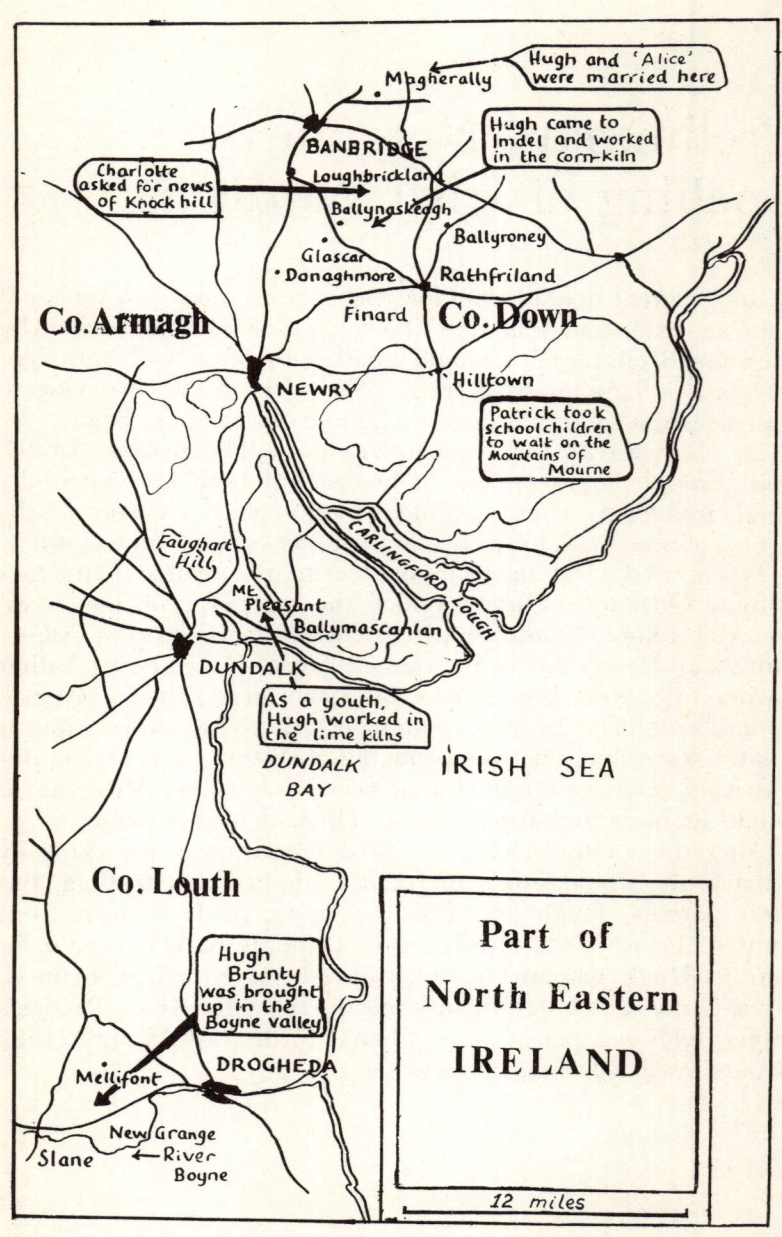

1 Introduction

'She was very shy and nervous, and spoke with a strong Irish accent', wrote Mary Taylor of her childhood friend Charlotte Brontë.[1] The strong Irish accent became a good deal softer over the years, and perhaps it was never quite as strong as Mary Taylor thought. On the other hand, it was probably much stronger than Charlotte either thought or wished. For her father, Patrick Brontë, had sought by every means in his power to lessen the burdens to be borne by a family who would have to admit the disreputable charge of Irish ancestry. He changed his name gradually over the years, from the Anglicised Irish 'Branty' to the cosmopolitan Bronté and then Brontë, symbolising his abandonment of Ireland, where he had spent his childhood, youth and young manhood.[2]

Amazingly little emphasis has been placed on this Irish heritage of the Brontë family. Some literary historians mention a Celtic temperament they discern in the work of Charlotte and Emily and the life of Branwell, but the majority of biographers begin their story in Liverpool or even at Cambridge, obviously considering Mr Brontë's past too shadowy or remote to be able to establish any precise facts or even probabilities about it. As in so many ways, they have been taken in by Mrs Gaskell and the information supplied to her by Mr Brontë himself, or perhaps have looked at the strength of the evidence for the early life and background of Patrick and decided the scholarship of the earlier biographers is much too suspect for any credence to be placed in it.

And, indeed, a great deal of painstaking detective work is necessary to confirm or disprove the vague legends that have been handed down to us about that remote period. Still, at the end of the twentieth century we are in some ways better placed to undertake this kind of work than the earlier writers were. We live in the age of the xerox, which can provide copies of rare nineteenth-century books so that they can be studied and mulled over in a way that used to be impossible. Techniques of local history study, folklore and genealogy are vastly improved. We have better texts of the Brontës' works, based on better manuscript sources. Brontë scholarship has advanced greatly since the publication of Wright's *The Brontës in Ireland* in 1893, and we also know much more about the personalities and vested interests of those who formed the Brontë establishment of the 1890s, and the generally Yorkshire-based orientation of those who made up the ranks of the Brontë Society.[3]

The quest we embark on in this book will be only partly a literary one. Its aim will be to discover the Irish background of the Brontë family and to see how far this background affected the life, thought patterns and literary expression of the sisters. So long as the Irish background remains unclear, any idea that it may have had an influence on the work may be dismissed or else pigeon-holed, without understanding, as vaguely Celtic.

We need to start by searching out and carefully documenting everything that is known about the Irish milieu in which Patrick Brontë grew up and in which his father had in turn grown up. We need, then, to turn to Patrick Brontë's own works, considerable portions of which reflect this milieu, and then we need to review the works of the sisters (and to a lesser extent Branwell) seeing if the characteristics of the father's work are represented in the work of the younger generation.

The reconstruction of this Irish milieu is a difficult but fascinating task. The evidence of witnesses is contradictory and partial, so that we need to check carefully the credentials of the various authorities. The quest will take us into some very odd corners: Irish social history, geography and religious attitudes will have to be considered, and we shall meet the claims and counter-claims of very partisan writers or story-tellers. Some of these are younger members of the Brontë family, who began to write letters to the press after the publication of *The Brontës in Ireland* and whose aims are in general two-fold: to claim kinship with Charlotte, who was an unusual person and a genius, but at the same time to show that there was nothing at all out of the ordinary about the Brontë family in County Down, who would all have been perfectly at home in a London drawing-room. The two aims were incompatible.

Among the concerns of the Irish in the late eighteenth and early nineteenth centuries were religious passion, rebellion and civil war, music and literature, education, ghosts and the supernatural and the tradition of oral story-telling. Since these concerns are prominent in the novels and poems of the Brontë sisters, it may well appear that an investigation into the parallels could be profitable. It is hardly necessary to point out that I am making no sweeping claims that all the Brontë novels are attributable to their origins. A large number of influences can be discerned in the works of the sisters, and I am suggesting no more than that the Irish background is one which has been a little overlooked.

There is only one place to start this work: Wright's *The Brontës in Ireland*. Though we shall certainly be making what we can of Patrick Brontë's carefully guarded and edited remarks made in a letter to Mrs Gaskell, a summary of which appears in *The Life of Charlotte Brontë*, these scraps of information are too pitifully scant to get us very far. Patrick Brontë did not want his past looked into. Only Wright looked into it, producing as a result a very readable and fluent book. This fluency won immediate praise, but within a year or two Wright was under sharp attack from Angus McKay, Horsfall Turner and the Brontë establishment headed by Clement Shorter. At first he defended himself with spirit, producing some new evidence. But sometimes this alleged evidence was so ludicrously and naïvely irrelevant that it could easily be refuted. Within six years of the publication of the book Wright had died, leaving behind the reputation of a romancer.

First of all, then, we must work carefully and critically through his book, trying to discover where his information came from, what foundation there may be in it, and what use Wright made of his sources. Everywhere we shall look for external evidence to corroborate details in the book. All the personages and dates mentioned, all the places and events, will be checked as far as possible against records of all sorts. If Wright's book is fiction, the people and places will vanish like the fairies about which Emily Brontë told her childhood stories. If there is any truth in it, we shall expect to find the places on maps and plans, the people in registers and on tax lists, the Presbyterian clergy in the *Fasti* and the buildings mentioned still in existence, albeit sometimes in ruins. Though he provides no bibliography, Wright does in fact give a lot of information about his sources. When these sources are examined the pattern that emerges is often one of overstatement and distortion, but never one of downright untruth.

As I have already suggested, there are two options open. We may decide *a priori* that Wright has nothing to offer, that his book is complete nonsense. Or we can approach the book in the belief that with all his faults Wright was the first in the field and indeed almost the only writer to give us any information about the Brontës' Irish background in the eighteenth and nineteenth centuries. In the end it will emerge that despite his errors and inconsistencies we should consider ourselves much indebted to Wright as providing the stimulus for investigations into the topic, and the one source, however frail, of evidence about the Brontë antecedents.

It will be convenient first to summarise Wright's story, then to look at the life and scholarly standing of the man himself. His sources will be carefully evaluated below.

According to Wright, Patrick Brontë's father, Hugh, had been adopted at an early age by a thoughtless and vengeful uncle named Welsh. This uncle constantly ill-treated him and caused him to run away from their home, a small-holding near the River Boyne, when he was about fifteen. He had run away to the neighbourhood of Dundalk, where he had taken employment in some lime-kilns. After a while he had formed friendships with some of the customers and had been introduced to a family in South Down named McClory. He fell in love with the daughter Eilís (Ayles, Alice or Eleanor). She was a Catholic, courted by a local farmer. However, she ran away with Hugh and they were married in a Protestant church at Magherally. They returned to the district of Eilís' birth, Ballynaskeagh. Here they took on the job of roasting corn, and in their small cottage Patrick Brontë was born in 1777.

Wright extends this story both forwards and backwards in time. The uncle, Welsh, was himself an orphan. He had been found on a boat travelling from Liverpool to Drogheda and had been adopted by Hugh's grandfather, but had acted like a cuckoo and turned the legitimate heirs out of the family home. Like Heathcliff, he had fallen in love with a daughter of the house, but unlike Heathcliff he had married her.

At the other end of the time scale, Wright gives many details of the Brontës in the nineteenth century, some of them sensational. He produces a mass of detail, in which he has been followed, for example, by John Cannon in *The Road to Haworth* and W. Haughton Crowe in *The Brontës of Ballynaskeagh*. The force of this chronicle is to link Patrick Brontë and the family at Haworth much more closely with Ireland than is discernible in most recent biographies, such as those of Winifred Gérin, Margot Peters or Phyllis Bentley. Our first task must be to consider the character, scholarly standing, sources and methods of Dr William Wright.

2 William Wright, Neighbour of the Brontës in Ireland

William Wright was born on 15 January 1837, the youngest child of William Wright, farmer, of Finard or Finnards, near Rathfriland, County Down. The greater part of his life was spent as a servant of the Presbyterian church, much of it overseas but some in England. His place of birth, spiritual allegiance, overseas service and academic competence are all matters highly relevant to a discussion of his account of the Irish Brontës. Before any judgement can be made on the value of his history, a little must be said about these matters.

The area in which Wright was born constitutes a sub-region of Ulster based on the market towns of Newry, Rathfriland and Banbridge. The terrain is undulating medium ground, dominated by the Mourne mountains to the south east and thus cut off from the sea. The towns are small and Belfast far enough away for its influence to be distanced. This geographical area is the same in which the Brunty (Brontë) family grew up, and when Wright records seeing roadmakers' carts with the Brontë name on the side during his childhood, he is telling the truth. Wright's acquaintance with the background of the Irish Brontës and the hamlets in which they lived may be said to be intimate. It is quite misleading to say as Elsie Harrison does, 'One Brontë enthusiast, named Wright, did indeed go to Ireland to rake over the ashes of the Brontë legend, but he turned up so confused a medley that, to the historian, his work seemed worthless.' Shorter is equally wrong to say, 'Dr Wright tells of many visits to Ireland in order to trace the Brontë traditions to their source', and as we shall see later he guesses wrongly when he suggests 'Dr Wright probably made his inquiries with the stories of Emily and Charlotte well in mind'.[1] Wright's birthplace is about three and a half miles across country from the birthplace of Patrick Brontë, and as we shall see, men whom

Wright claims as informants of his many years before Emily and Charlotte wrote their stories can be shown to have been in a position to know what Wright claimed.

Wright was a Presbyterian. He was probably educated at the Belfast Royal Academical Institution, though no record of him has survived.[2] From there he went on to Queen's College, Belfast, matriculating in 1858 and obtaining a BA degree. In 1859 he entered the Belfast Presbyterian College. In 1864 he was licensed by the Belfast Presbytery and ordained a missionary to Damascus in 1865. After spending ten years in the Middle East he returned to the British Isles and to an honorary doctorate at Glasgow. While in the East he had become an adept at writing in his capacity as correspondent of the *Pall Mall Gazette*. From 1876 until the end of his life he was the Editorial Superintendent of the British and Foreign Bible Society. In later years he lived near London and devoted himself in part to writing, producing books on diverse topics of a religious nature or about travel in the Middle East. He had played a significant part, as an amateur, in defining the origin of some Hittite inscriptions, but he is not to be confused with another Dr William Wright, a professional Orientalist.

We may nevertheless note how well Wright impressed learned people with whom he came in contact. James Robertson, Professor of Oriental Languages at Glasgow, was a prime mover in recommending Wright for the Honorary DD in 1882. He wrote a long note in support of a motion to confer the degree, making the following interesting points:

(i) He quotes from Professor E. H. Palmer of Cambridge concerning Wright's very rapid and elegant mastery of Arabic. 'I can testify to the great facility as well as the scholarlike elegance with which he preached', Palmer wrote.

(ii) Wright was constantly cited by the Palestine Exploration Fund, expressing its indebtedness to him for help in its researches.

(iii) Dr Samuel Davidson had written, 'If I was asked to recommend any English scholar to the attention of the Senators of your University, I should at once mention Mr Wright as one on whom the degree of D.D. might be worthily conferred.'

(iv) Wright is said to have used 'ingenious arguments'; to have been 'fearless and searching' and to have employed 'indomitable perseverance' in the cause of Bible publication.³

This testimonial letter gives a picture of Wright consistent with what we know of him from other sources and from his book. There is no doubt of his energy and intellectual curiosity, nor his determination in the face of difficulty. He showed determination in obtaining the relaxation of Turkish attitudes to Christians, and apparently did so without antagonising Turkish leaders. His involvement with the Hamalite stones shows both curiosity and persistence, and reminds us of his undergraduate attempts to discover the Brontë origins in Southern Ireland. In both enterprises he was energetic and unorthodox.

The speed and completeness with which Wright learned Arabic is interesting. Besides a gift for language which is reflected in the pleasing style of *The Brontës in Ireland*, an extensive memory is argued, together with a strong ability to make himself understood by a completely alien people, and to understand them. The warmth of tone in Robertson's letter suggests that Wright had a natural capacity to get on with all kinds of men. This energy, curiosity, excellent memory and versatile understanding should all be taken into account when we come to judge the truth of his Brontë history. On the other hand, we do not find in Wright's record any intense or close study of a scholarly kind: his method used intuition, charm, lengthy and capacious but perhaps inaccurate memory, and elegant language.

Wright's political views perhaps stemmed from his Presbyterianism. He is attacked by J. Ramsden for intruding these views into his book on the Brontës, and there may be some reason for this attack.⁴ Wright's disapproval of the Papacy, shown in *The Power Behind the Pope*, does not make him a Unionist or even a strong Royalist. We may note that both Catholic and Presbyterian had been unacceptable to the English-oriented Church of Ireland, and that in Ulster Presbyterian ministers had been in the forefront of the 1798 rebellion. Like many Nonconformists these Presbyterians made good missionaries, and Wright's book partakes of polemic as part of his Presbyterian heritage. It is quite natural that he should look most favourably on his own denomination, but one notes too his friendly feeling for the

Catholic clergy and for a new generation of Church of Ireland ministers represented by such people as Thomas Tighe. Above all, we note the prominence given to Irish Nationalism, not indeed in the modern sense, but in the approval given to land reformers whose ideas are perhaps naïvely put into the mouth of Hugh Brunty. Wright understood the Ulster peasant because he was an Ulster peasant, albeit relatively high in the social scale. He is unlikely to be far wrong in judging the motives or feelings of his chief characters. Wright is an Irishman and an Ulsterman, not recognising any conflict between these two, and his book contains a due measure of Irish pride in the Brontës coupled with Nonconformist missionary endeavour to reveal as truth the unrevealed facts about the origin of Brontë genius which will put South Down on the literary map.

Wright, then, was born and brought up within four or five miles of all the main scenes of the story of Hugh Brunty and his brilliant son Patrick: Imdel, where Patrick was born, Glascar, where he taught in the school, Rathfriland where he borrowed books from Samuel Barber, Loughorne where Hugh is said to have worked as a labourer, Ballynaskeagh manse where an early copy of *Jane Eyre* was read by anxious Irish uncles of Charlotte, the Knock hill about which Charlotte enquired when her uncle visited Haworth. Throughout his life, even before the Brontës were famous, his eager but slightly uncritical interest in anthropology and antiquarianism was storing yarns and facts about the family. He was twenty when the first account of Charlotte Brontë's life was published by Mrs Gaskell, but even then he had gathered together a farrago of tales concerning her ancestry, which at that time he had no means or intention of sharing with any public.

3 An Irish Presbyterian Milieu

Addressing the Brontë Society in May 1895, Wright told the members that he had 'penned most of his book when he was about sixteen years of age'. In one of the chapters of his series of articles for *McClure's Magazine* he says that the account of the Brontë ceilidh was written out as a composition exercise.[1] At first his interest had nothing to do with literary history at all. He was intrigued by the 'living legend' of an unusual family, whose appearance and lifestyle set them apart from other inhabitants of his part of South Down at the time. They appeared to preserve artistic and folk-customs which were becoming rare. Wright's view of the Irish Brontës as a group set apart from their neighbours in Ballynaskeagh is supported by a number of witnesses, though some try to play the differences down. But John Brontë of Wellington, New Zealand, wrote to Wright to say that the Brontës were a 'peculiar family, quite different from the ordinary folk in their intellectual grasp'.[2]

The first step in our bid to test Wright's book in detail requires an examination of his informants one by one, so far as possible chronologically, so that we may see whether they could have had the opportunity to get to know the alleged facts they retailed to him. The first of them nursed William Wright in childhood. She had lived 'within a quarter of a mile of their home' and had a store of wild tales to tell about them.[3] Wright describes her as 'my kind old nurse' who gave him 'much Bronte lore'.[4] She was 'a close relative' of a certain Kaly Nesbit, but is herself unnamed. It seems probable that she would be looking after the little William when he was about three or four. She must have employed stories she had heard from the Brontës as fairy tales, though it is unclear whether these would be the classic Ulster tales which Hugh Brunty seems to have known, or the more localised yarns concerning the exploits of members of the family in the glens and fields of Ballynaskeagh. Wright's acquaintance with his nurse could perhaps be dated about 1840 or 1841. It is hardly necessary to say that at this time the Brontë sisters had published nothing, under their own names or any other.

It is almost certainly possible to identify 'Kaly' Nesbit from Glascar registers. His name seems to be short for 'Caleb', a Christian name used only once at Glascar. His first and apparently only child was baptised on 22 May 1803. She was Margaret, and may well have been Wright's nurse. If so, she would be in her late thirties when he was in her care. If Caleb Nesbit married at the average time for Glascar members, he would have been born about 1775–80, and was thus a contemporary of Patrick Brontë. The stories told to Wright by his nurse would be the same that Patrick heard from Hugh. Caleb Nesbit's cottage was at Imdel.

One of the most important of Wright's informants was his next acquaintance, William McAlister. We shall have cause to refer to him and his family frequently. It will emerge that the relatives of Wright's 'first classical teacher' lived close to the Brontës and almost certainly influenced the life of Patrick in various ways. William McAlister was born at Derrydrummuck, the next townland to Glascar, and baptised at the chapel on 5 July 1801. He was the second son of Samuel McAlister, his elder brother John having been born in 1798. His mother's maiden name was Maxwell.[5] Wright describes the family as 'freeholders and local gentry in a small way', much involved with the administration of Glascar church. As we shall see later, the family appears to have been the *most* influential at Glascar, and to have been the biggest landholders in the several townlands of the area; however, they were not precisely freeholders in the English sense. They continued to live in the district, John McAlister eventually farming land near Ballynaskeagh cross-roads.

By now we have come some way from Elsie Harrison's 'One Brontë enthusiast... [raking] over the ashes of the Brontë legend.' According to Wright, Samuel McAlister had heard Hugh Brunty tell the tales of his youth in the Brontë kiln shortly after Patrick's birth. In 1836 a Samuel McAlister is recorded as the occupier of Derrydrummuck mill. This seems likely to be William's father himself, and his trade explains why he was in the Brontë corn-kiln at night.[6] Unfortunately, we have no means of knowing Samuel's age, but if he married at the normal age for Glascar members, he may have been born about 1770, and was thus a child of about eight when he originally heard

Hugh's stories. He might actually remember, as a child, the sensation caused by Hugh's arrival in the district and courtship of Eilís; but his memory would not necessarily be accurate in all respects. The close proximity in which the McAlisters lived with the Bruntys gives us general confidence in Wright's story, but it is slightly less encouraging that on page 8 he talks of his tutor's 'brilliant imagination'.

A later writer describes William McAlister as 'one of the most brilliant men of his day the Presbyterian church in Ireland has ever possessed'. He was 'a little dark man . . . of indomitable energy and a tender heart . . . original and good-humoured and jovial . . . pious without being straight-laced or sanctimonious'.[7] This endearing character clearly made a great impression on Wright. Part of his system of education was to make his pupil retell Hugh Brunty's stories until he knew them by heart. His career is worth investigating.

Educated at the Belfast Royal Academical Institution, McAlister (described at the time as of 'Aghaderg') obtained the Institution's General Certificate in 1824. He was ordained a Presbyterian minister in 1826 and given the charge of Clarkesbridge, where he remained until 1850.[8] In that year he moved to Ryans at Finard. Here he met the young Wright, who would have been about the same age as his own five children. McAlister's main aim in teaching Classics was the elaboration of the pupils' English. He would sometimes 'give me the plot of such works as the *Hecuba* or the *Alcestis* and leave me to fill in the wording in my own way'. When Greek plots ran out McAlister would use stories told by Hugh Brunty. Some of these were in McAlister's view 'just as striking and worthy to be recounted as the wrath of Achilles or the wanderings of Pius Æneas'.[9] Wright's task was to write the stories, or sometimes tell them 'with as much spirit as possible', since dullness was the only quality intolerable to McAlister. Nothing is said here about truth.

Wright's remarkable account of how he came to know Hugh Brunty's stories laid him open to the charge of fictionalising true stories, or at best of retelling legend with no more firm basis than the story of *Alcestis*. He does not seem to recognise this problem sufficiently in the book, and assumes that McAlister saw Hugh Brunty's stories as literal fact, though he can hardly have thought the same about the Greek myths. However, it may be that McAlister had recognised the similarity between Celtic legend and Greek. It must be remembered that at the beginning of the nineteenth century Irish language and literature was not so firmly proscribed in its own land as it later became.

Hugh Brunty evidently knew many stories, not only the one about his own life which assumes such prominence in *The Brontës in Ireland*. Wright follows his teacher in likening these to Classical myth, and later compares Hugh to the Arabian storytellers whom he has seen during his service with the British and Foreign Bible Society in the Middle East. Unlike most of his readers, he seems to have understood the notion of the seanchaí, though he gives no other Irish examples. Later, we shall try to discover what stories Hugh may have told. Wright has no agreed terminology for dealing with Celtic oral literature, and cannot rely on any understanding of the topic from his audience. Indeed he does not seem to know anything of Irish native literature. This has the effect of making his information seem garbled, but on the other hand, since he is describing both this and the Irish folk tradition from his own observation and acquaintance, we can rule out the possibility that he had read of these art forms in books and transferred them to Hugh Brunty. There never were more inexpert accounts of folk-customs or Irish literary productions; but their very naïvety makes them the more strongly confirmed.

McAlister had heard Hugh Brunty tell his stories in person, though it is worth noting that when this happened Hugh Brunty must have been very old and McAlister very young.[10] It is thought that Hugh died about 1808 (though this is very tentative dating) at which time McAlister would have been seven. The tales seem to have been reinforced by McAlister's father's reminiscences from the corn-kiln. Even if William McAlister did not recall all the details of the stories, it is quite likely that he retained a good deal. It is unlikely that Hugh's story of his own life was unvarnished, but Wright seems to say that accounts of it were widespread, and adduces four witnesses to support it, though unfortunately without naming any. When Hugh tries to penetrate further into the past, he is perhaps mythologising, as we shall see. But in telling the story of his life Hugh was doing no more nor less than many a seanchaí in a culture where ancestry and the past were important.

By the time Wright published *The Brontës in Ireland* William McAlister was dead. He may have been consulted during the writing process, which apparently took Wright some time. McAlister had retired in 1875 and lived near Warrenpoint until 1879. We do not precisely know how often Wright returned to Ireland after his tour of duty in the Middle East. Certainly he had relatives there still, though they may not have been close ones. He does not positively refer in the book to any recent consultation with McAlister. This is discouraging but not fatal.

There are a few indications of first-hand knowledge of the Irish Brontës on the part of Wright dating from mid century, though he tends to exaggerate them. At one point he claims to have seen Patrick himself, on a visit. This possibility will need consideration later. His next burst of interest in the Brontës was when he was a student. It was at this time that he became intimate with David McKee, Presbyterian minister of Annaclone, who lived in Ballynaskeagh manse. Wright eventually married McKee's daughter. The precise date when Wright became a pupil of McKee's is uncertain. It has proved impossible to find for certain what school Wright attended, and it may be that his pre-college education was partly in McKee's hands. It should be remembered that Mrs Gaskell's biography of Charlotte Brontë dates from 1857, and this seems to have provided an impetus for Wright's strange researches. However, it is reported that he was telling 'Brontë stories' in his undergraduate days, and this corroborates his assertion that the Brontës were no new interest for him.[11] One of the oddest things Wright did at this time was to dress as a peasant and take to the roads in the south of Ireland. What he found there we shall see later.

There are many strands to this part of the story and they need examining in isolation. From this time dates the extraordinary assertion that *Jane Eyre* was sent to Ireland in the first edition, read by the Irish Brontës, taken to Mr McKee, and when approved by him, accepted by the relatives. It must be said at once that this does not square with the note in Patrick Brontë's handwriting in the 1853 edition sent by him to his brother Hugh Brontë.[12] The note reads:

> To Mr Hugh Brontè, Ballynasceaugh, near Rathfriland, Ireland – This is the first work; published by my Daughter – Under the fictitious name of 'Currer Bell' – which is the [erasure] usual way – at first by Authors, but her real name is everywhere known – She sold the copyright of this and her

other two works for fifteen hundred pounds – so that she has to pay for the books she gets, the same as others – Her other two books, are in six volumes, and would cost nearly four pounds – This was formerly in three volumes – In two years hence, when all shall be published in a cheaper form, I may send them – You can let my brothers and sisters, read this – P Brontë, A. B. Incumbent of Haworth near Keighley: Jany.20th 1853 –

If a first edition of *Jane Eyre* had gone to Ireland, surely Patrick would have known of this? Wright suggests that Charlotte might send a copy without telling her father. As we shall see, Charlotte's attitude to the Irish Brontës and to the Irish in general at the time does not make this likely. It looks much more as if Wright, and perhaps David McKee in reminiscing, had mistaken the exact nature of the volume that had been sent. Perhaps the very exciting receipt of a copy of a first *cheap* edition of a bestseller by an authoress whose father was a native of the area, well known to many people, has been exaggerated to become the receipt of a first edition, which might be no less exciting to the Irish Brontës and to David McKee. For our present purpose the incident is worth noting for the light it throws on Wright's methods and motives: it is hard to believe that his information was subjected by him to sceptical scrutiny, and the importance of the event may have been exaggerated to make it more impressive. But the book sent was a real one, not a figment of the imagination.

The arrival of *Jane Eyre* at Ballynaskeagh was a shock to the Brontë uncles. Hugh Brontë is said by Wright to have brought the volume with its pages uncut to McKee's manse. It was read immediately and in full, while Hugh waited anxiously, drinking the tea which had been provided for him. Wright's witnesses for this episode include David McKee himself and the girl who was later to become Mrs Wright.[13] There can be little doubt that the winter scene at the manse is correctly described, but wrongly dated to 1848 instead of 1853. Later, we shall see what Mr McKee thought of *Jane Eyre*.

Hearing this story on his visit to Ballynaskeagh in 1855 or thereabouts Wright seems to have been reminded of his early interest in the curious Brontë clan. At this time he would have a great deal of testimony from eye-witnesses to draw on. He claims to have talked to Hugh about his trip to England. This must have been about this time, since Hugh died in 1863. It must be remembered that denials by members of later generations of the Brontë family in Ireland about events known to Hugh and Patrick Brontë's other brothers may not have the authority of Wright's own narrative. These denials and comments date from the 1890s, whereas Wright talked to Hugh Brontë and others who had known the family thirty or more years before. For example, Charlotte's 'last remaining cousin', Rose Heslip, whom we shall meet later, said she had never heard the story of Welsh, the 'strange child' found on a Liverpool to Ireland boat and later to become the 'wicked uncle' of Hugh Brunty: 'My uncle Welsh was a constant visitor, but I never heard it once named among them.'[14]

Mrs Heslip may have been muddled by the name 'Welsh'; but ignorance of the 'strange child' story by her uncle does not prove that William McAlister's memory of the tale told by Hugh Brunty is unsound. On the other hand, we do not know how far Wright may have kept written notes at this time, apart from his composition exercises, or whether his understanding of evidential considerations was any better in talking to Hugh Brontë Jr than when talking about the 1853 *Jane Eyre* to the McKees.

The most *outré* yarn apparently picked up from the McKee milieu about 1855–8 concerns the visit to England of Hugh Brontë Jr with a shillelagh, with the aim of cudgelling some sense into the head of the reviewer in the *Quarterly* who had damned *Jane Eyre*. Wright gives his authority for this story as Mr McKee, via his daughter, Mrs Wright. An enormous air of secrecy surrounded the story, it seems. Hugh Brontë would tell the story at first hand neither to Miss McKee nor Wright himself and the account quoted on page 292 of *The Brontës in Ireland* has the ring of truth. When asked for corroboration and told that McKee had relayed the story, Hugh Brontë Jr replied 'Then you don't need to hear of it from me'. The whole question of this story's authenticity will be raised again when we consider various visits of the Irish family to England. Certainly there are grave problems about the story, but difficulties also about dismissing it.

Wright's third foray into Brontë country occurred after he returned from the Middle East in 1875. Though now he seems to have lived in England instead of Ireland, he had by this time gained some repute as a writer through his despatches to the *Pall Mall Gazette* and his work on behalf of the British and Foreign Bible Society. During the 1880s he received his honorary doctorate at Glasgow and published several books. His confidence in writing the account of the Irish Brontës was increased and his estimation of the value of such work enhanced by new Brontë commentaries such as those by Birrell, Wemyss Reid and A. M. F. Robinson. He renewed contact with Ireland and with such members of the Brontë family as remained. The group was depleted, and Wright would deal through third parties such as the Revd Henry Lett and the Revd J. B. Lusk.

Henry Lett was the incumbent at Aghaderg, the parish which included Glascar and Ballynaskeagh. Lett discovered and made available to Wright the old parish register of Drumballyroney. The register is still extant and the Brontë entries have several times been reproduced. A facsimile of one page is given in Cannon's *The Road to Haworth*. Lett arrived at Aghaderg in 1886 and found the register on show at an exhibition in Banbridge Court House during the summer of 1889.[15] J. B. Lusk was the Presbyterian minister at Glascar, who diligently followed the clues given by Wright and unearthed a good deal of supporting material, including some books that had belonged to Patrick Brontë, which will be mentioned later. Lusk came to Haworth in January 1897 and in a talk to the Brontë Society 'confirmed Dr Wright's narrative back to the point in time where Hugh came to Mount Pleasant lime kilns'.[16] He would not give an opinion on whether Hugh's story of his own childhood was true or false but 'That Hugh Brontë told it there could be no manner of doubt. . . . Hugh's children certainly knew the story.' Lusk had excellent opportunities of talking to the oldest inhabitants in Glascar and the loss of his notebooks is to be regretted.

Lusk's influence had been important, not only in securing the documentary evidence contained in the books mentioned, but in talking patiently to old Alice Brontë (Patrick's sister), who had survived all her brothers and sisters and had thus emerged in an era when everything to do with the family was of crucial interest. She had eked out her living with a small pension, granted not by Smith, Elder, as some thought, but by Pargeter's Old Maids charity in Birmingham.[17] Lusk may also have been the means through whom Wright contacted some Brontës of later generations: in particular Rose Heslip and Maggie Shannon. Their

evidence was ambivalent and they only came to the fore after the
Brontë story had been published, but Wright knew both of
them while he was putting the finishing touches to his book and
they contributed elements of it.

J. B. Lusk's unpublished notes were tapped by an anonymous
writer to *The Banbridge Chronicle* for 7 September 1918. He
corroborated Wright's long interest in the family, and says he
'used to tell Brontë stories at College'. While investigating the
Brontë background, Lusk had been warned to keep away, and
been told they were 'the wildest, most outlandish and godless lot'
that ever lived in a Christian land. (The letter writer had himself
met a neighbour of the Brontës 'a few days ago', who 'reflected
the awe felt by the people of Ballynaskeagh for the strange
family'.) Lusk considered that old Hugh Brunty had been in the
habit of telling his family history, 'if not with the completeness
Dr Wright has given it, at any rate in its main features'. He
alleged that Alice Brontë had given him 'the kernel' of it in an
interview, though it may seem that the kernel is a small one in
comparison with Wright's nut.

The unpublished notes quoted in the letter reveal two main
points of corroboration of Wright. First, the wildness of the
Brontë uncles is displayed in a further word-picture of the
evening when young Welsh Brontë was drowned in the Bann
during 1833: 'They went along the road to meet the corpse
tearing their hair and wailing with loud long-drawn cries.'

Lusk's other corroborative evidence concerns the Brontës'
religious affiliations.

> I had people tell me that they were all Roman Catholics and
> only became Protestants when Patrick was ordained in the
> English Church. . . . One of the many riots that 12th of July
> celebrations formerly led to in that locality was celebrated in
> rough verses that are still remembered. The Brontës, with
> their mother . . . seem to have taken the Catholic side in the
> fray.

Here the letter-writer quotes the following:

> But the Brontë boys they feared no noise
> And why should they do so?

Lusk was told by a number of informants that James Brontë had applied unsuccessfully to join first a 'ribbon' (Catholic) lodge, then an Orange lodge. Eilís Brontë's adherence to 'her husband's' religion was only nominal, Lusk concludes. The religious position of the Brontës in Ulster will be considered at a later stage; meanwhile we note that there are possible antecedents here for Emily's refusal to be tied down to any particular religious sect. Lusk's notes were, of course, obtained before the main flood of Brontë biographical work in the mid-1890s.

One of Wright's contemporaries in the Glascar area was William John McCracken. By the time Wright began to consider producing a book on the Brontës, McCracken was the minister at Ballyeaston Presbyterian church, Belfast. He had been baptised at Glascar in January 1836 and like Wright had been tutored by the Revd David McKee.[18] He had entered college at the same time as Wright, and after a tour of duty in Monaghan had taken up his ministry in Belfast in 1878. It seems likely that he had kept in close touch with some of his relations in Glascar and Ballynaskeagh. It was McCracken who rediscovered and identified the Brontë kiln, the small cottage where Patrick Brontë had been born. He could remember stories about the Brontë family told by his mother. Born Elizabeth Wilson, she had been one of Patrick's pupils at Glascar. According to Wright she was six at the time of the 1798 rebellion. It seems likely that a good deal of what Wright tells us about Patrick's time at Glascar and his methods of teaching may have been told by Elizabeth to her son.

As Wright's notes neared book form he seems to have approached various old inhabitants of the Aghaderg district. He mentions Paddy McClory, a servant of David McKee, who is apparently the source of detail about the testing of Hugh Brunty when he wished to marry Eilís. There must be some reservations here, as the event occurred in 1776 and however old Paddy McClory may have been he cannot have been an eye-witness. Still, in this kind of small country community elements of truth live on in legend. Wright also relies on an old man named Frazer (whose accuracy he doubts enough to change his version of the story of the battle between Welsh Brontë and Sam Clarke), Hugh Norton, and the two Todd brothers. The Todds of the 1770s are said to be among the customers at Dundalk lime-kilns.

Hugh Norton, born about 1803, was of the generation of William McAlister. His existence is corroborated in Glascar registers, in which three of his children are recorded at their baptisms in 1831–5. If he knew Hugh Brunty, this would have been when he was very young and Hugh old.[19] However, it may be significant that people who were children at the time of Hugh's final years did remember him. The story-telling faculty would be appreciated by them, and they would have both the time to listen and the imagination to accept the stories. Horsfall Turner says sternly of Norton that his 'stories may suit a Captain Mayne Reid, but they are inadmissible as strict biography'. Norton's two main contributions are reminiscences of Hugh Brunty mending fences and talking philosophically as he worked, and the story of the ghost which haunted the glen opposite the Brontës' houses. A cluster of episodes connected with ghosts were corroborated by younger Brontë generations, and we shall see that though this was done half-jokingly, Patrick's brothers did take part in dabbling with the supernatural. Horsfall Turner's strictures are therefore a little high minded and typical of those late nineteenth-century writers who wished to see the Brontës as respectable English writers whose peasant ancestry in Ireland could be written off.

Though Captain Mayne Reid was born in Ballyroney, and Wright says in his introduction that he had a considerable knowledge of the Brontës, no single incident in the book is ascribed to Mayne Reid's memory. It is possible that he may have played a part in telling Wright some tales of the Brunty past, but it is by now impossible to discover any evidence of this.

I have so far said little about one of Wright's main sources of information, the man who became his father-in-law, the Revd David McKee.[20] McKee was born in the same year as Patrick Brontë. Though he came from County Down, it seems likely that his birthplace was in the neighbourhood of Hillsborough or Annahilt, some twelve miles to the north of Imdel. He spent some of his youth in Ballynahinch, where we shall later meet one of Patrick's brothers at the main local battle in the 1798 uprising. McKee is said to have watched the battle. His younger sister, Margaret, had married a farmer of Ballynahinch whose name was Edgar. Wright's story that McKee, then aged twenty-one, held in his arms on that occasion a baby who would grow up to be a temperance leader is quite consistent with what we discover from external sources of Dr John Edgar (1798–1866), a major Belfast temperance reformer. Unfortunately, the area of McKee's birth is rather distant for us to suppose he had first-hand acquaintance with the Brunty family or story until he came to Ballynaskeagh in 1804. By this time Patrick had left for England, but Hugh Brunty was still alive and apparently regarded as a local character.

The Yorkshire writer J. Ramsden is very flippant about McKee's eccentricity, but all other writers speak with great enthusiasm of his lively mind and breadth of knowledge. As I have already suggested, he may not have been literary man enough to distinguish a first edition from a first cheap edition, but he was certainly no man's fool. As a farmer as well as minister – he once told a neighbour 'If you would thrash a little and dig a little it would do you good' – he had a reputation for talking to everyone in the district and would give away his own clothes to beggars.[21] The local Catholic priest was on good terms with him. He was a member of a literary group which subscribed to Sir Walter Scott's novels as they came out. His teaching of the Classics to pupils who came to Ballynaskeagh manse was inspired rather than thoroughgoing. 'I have rarely heard anything in the way of translation more enjoyable than the rush and vigour of his translation of a battle scene from the Iliad', said a former pupil.[22] We can see that such a man might well inspire Wright's curiosity about the Brontës and their legend, but might not be too concerned to check the precise publishing date of a copy of *Jane Eyre*.

At this point we may perhaps stand back a little to evaluate these sources of our knowledge about the eighteenth- and early nineteenth-century Brontës in Ireland. We have discovered that our mediator, William Wright, was brought up as a child among the small village communities of County Down where the brothers and sisters of Patrick Brontë were still living. A number of his informants certainly knew Hugh Brunty and listened to his stories, but only when they were children. One of his best informants, a close friend and contemporary, W. J. McCracken, had a mother who was taught by Patrick at Glascar school, while another influential informant, William McAlister, was the son of a miller, Samuel McAlister, who was some years older than Patrick and who had every opportunity to hear Hugh's stories during corn-roasting sessions at the Brontë kiln. McAlister Jr was a well-educated man, versed in the Classics, but lacking in sceptical objectivity and possessed of a noted imagination. David McKee, another contemporary of Patrick, may have arrived on the scene at Ballynaskeagh just too late to meet Patrick himself, but his character suggests that he would communicate very readily with the local population and soon hear local legends and gossip. David McKee was Wright's father-in-law.

It can hardly be doubted that Wright's garbled and possibly exaggerated story has some basis. As early as the 1840s he got to know the people who had known Hugh Brunty, and his undergraduate enquiries made during the 1850s cannot be dismissed out of hand. His investigation was never logical or scientific, and he spent a lot of time on wild-goose chases. But this does not diminish his evidence to the point of extinction. We must take Wright seriously, and make what we can of the material he provides about the milieu in which the 'eccentrick' father of the Brontës grew up.

4 The Brontë Sensation and its Reception

When *The Brontës in Ireland* appeared in 1893 its reception was rapturous. A version had already been printed in *McClure's Magazine* but little publicity had been accorded to it. Now a new light was shining on the 'Brontë genius' and Wright did not moderate his claims for the strength of the light. Genius was hereditary; the Brontës had genius; they had inherited it from their Irish ancestors. One part of Wright's motive was to display the source of this genius. But other readers discovered other motives. The Presbyterian Wright was using the Irish Brontës to further several of his own causes, notably Temperance, Irish Home Rule and Presbyterianism. Subsidiary to the Brontë story there does run through the book a thread of Irish nationalism, seen in the detailed propositions for the 'Tenant Right' cause, ascribed to Hugh Brunty, an emphasis on Presbyterianism to the detriment of the influence of the Church of Ireland, perhaps felt by Wright to be of an English complexion, and a dislike of drink. It is worth bearing in mind these biases when judging the deeds ascribed to the Irish Brontës; their allegiance to churches other than Presbyterian may be played down, their attitude to drink will be a sensitive matter, and they may be shown as Irish nationalists. On the other hand, we shall see that an attacker whose political and religious stance was against these attitudes may underestimate the book on its factual side.

Controversies and discussions over the book reached a peak in 1895–7 in *The Sketch*, *The Academy*, *The Westminster Review* and *The Bookman*. Books and pamphlets sparked off by Wright included those by Ramsden, McKay and Turner, and Clement Shorter's *Charlotte Brontë and her Circle* also made reference to the new discoveries.[1] Andrew Lang suggested that Wright would do best to support his story of Hugh Brunty by the discovery of a few Brontë tombstones, thus showing he did not understand the stratum of society from which Hugh Brunty emanated. McKay purported to have great interest in the Brontës, but the beginning of his *Westminster Review* article is odd. He says that he was naturally interested 'As a Brontë enthusiast' when the book came out, but that his curiosity 'died down' when many laudatory reviews were printed. 'Recently I procured this volume for the purpose of keeping my Brontë knowledge up to date', he goes on, and it was then that he found the book unsatisfactory. It seems strange that this 'Brontë enthusiast' didn't read a new and sensational book until two years after its publication.[2]

Like his successor, Ramsden, McKay seems only interested in finding fault with Wright's book, though in doing so both unearth new material from among the Brontë relatives. Meanwhile Wright himself goes off at a tangent and with the aid of a Mr David Martin of Newry claims to discover the origin of the Brontës in the shape of an old ferryman from Lough Erne named Frank Prunty who remembered that his ancestors had come from Galway, but changed the name of the town to Drogheda when this was suggested to him.[3] The evidential link between Frank Prunty and the Bruntys of County Down is minimal, and neither his photograph nor his signature help in any way to answer questions about Hugh Brunty's origin, though they damage Wright's credibility. It is now time to turn to some of the Brontë family themselves, who commented on Wright's book and gave further small details to McKay, Turner and Ramsden, or whose late communications to Wright were printed by him in letters or articles in some of the magazines mentioned above.

Patrick Brontë had nine siblings. The dates of baptism of six are recorded in the register of Drumballyroney church, mentioned above. It is necessary to enumerate them briefly now, and return for details later. The brothers were William, who married and whose family emigrated to New Zealand and other places; Hugh, who did not marry; James, who did not marry either; and Welsh, who had three children and whose descendants stayed in Northern Ireland. The sisters were Jane, who died at the age of thirty; Mary; Rose, about whom little is known; Sarah, who seems to have made a runaway marriage with a Simon Collins and whose name was known to Charlotte Brontë (her daughter Rose later became Mrs Heslip); and Alice, who did not marry but survived to the age of ninety-five and was thus available for her comments when Wright was checking his data. Hugh Jr was known to Wright and many memories of him remained in the 1890s, whether or not he took his shillelagh to London. James led an active life, and certainly visited Haworth; Welsh was thought of as very gentlemanly, but his sons were unlucky; and William fought for the United Irishmen in the 1798 rising.

Those who added to the story on the publication of Wright's book were

    (i) *John Brontë*, a grandson of William, at that time a chemist in New Zealand, whose letter of 24 October 1894 was published in *The Bookman*.
    (ii) *Maggie Shannon*, who with her sister lived near Lisnacreevy and wrote to Wright, McKay, to a Belfast newspaper, and gave an interview to Ramsden.[4]
    (iii) *Rose Heslip*, who was living at Heckmondwike, Yorks, in the 1890s and died there on 15 March 1915 about three weeks after the second wife of the Revd A. B. Nicholls died in Banagher, Kings County (Offaly).[5]

These were children of descendants respectively of William, Welsh and Sarah. As previously mentioned, very important was the evidence of

    (iv) *Alice Brontë*, who gave information to the Revd J. B. Lusk and perhaps direct to Wright also, and who died on 15 January 1891.[6]

It may be supposed that where their evidence agrees, and sometimes where it does not, these close relatives of Patrick are correctly recalling events as far back as the last and even the penultimate decade of the eighteenth century. Alice, for example, remembered both her father and mother, though not a great deal about her father's legendary gifts. It will be as well here to recount the information given by these Brontë descendants and begin to evaluate it.

Alice was clear that her father, Hugh Brunty, came from Drogheda.[7] She said his uncle had taken him from his father's place when he was eight. But later his aunt had a child and so Hugh was displaced in their affections. Though slight, this information precisely corroborates Wright's yarn heard from McAlister.

By the time of her death Alice Brontë was a member of the Church of Ireland. Her obituary in the *Banbridge Chronicle* makes it clear that she had attended Aghaderg parish church once the family moved into Ballynaskeagh.[8] However, Aghaderg was some way off, and one wonders if her attendance could have been very regular, at least in later days. The incumbent of Aghaderg, H. W. Lett, helped to conduct her funeral.

The *Banbridge Chronicle* records Alice's interesting accent: 'It had a Scottish flavour for which the inhabitants were formerly remarkable.' Reference to this accent is made by other writers, and the matter needs consideration later. To talk with Alice Brontë, the newspaper goes on, was like talking to 'the last minstrel'. It is not clear what is meant by this, but it may seem that the reporter is trying to convey an air of distinction about the old lady, and perhaps something bardic in her demeanour or utterance. We may note that Patrick Brontë also impressed callers at Haworth by his 'old fashioned courtesy', which in part seems to have consisted of gallant expressions and high-flown diction. This style of English, which in our day might be thought pompous, is much like the loquacious Irish Gælic of the eigtheenth-century poets of whom we shall be hearing.

Alice remembered her mother, after whom she was named. She had told Wright that her mother was fair-haired and her father sandy, and that her mother had lived longer than her father, though dates are highly speculative.[9] She had said her father was not very tall but stout; though several other Brontës were remembered for their height. It is interesting that she did not think of her father as grey-haired, and perhaps this strengthens the notion that he died without reaching old age.

John Brontë was a New Zealand pharmacist, the great-nephew of Patrick Brontë, and a grandson of William Brontë. He may have written to Wright during the time when *The Brontës in Ireland* was being compiled.[10] He later wrote to *The Bookman* giving general assent to what Wright had written. Concerning Hugh Brunty's story of Welsh the usurper he is silent, though his congratulation in general to Wright 'on the treatment of the history of my ancestors' suggests that he did not dissent. His other evidence concerns the character of the family in Ireland as he knew it, and the links between County Down and Haworth. He was born in 1834/5 and could therefore remember Patrick's generation, though not that of the elder Hugh and Eilís.

John corroborates the involvement of William Brontë with the 1798 rebellion of the United Irishmen and the battle at Ballynahinch in language which describes the scene of pursuit and concealment just as if it were an exploit of Gondal rebels.

> [William] had crossed over the bogs and marshes, making a beeline for County Armagh, and swam through the canal, while the horsemen had to keep the roads and bridges, and . . . as the shades of evening fell he took refuge on a hill covered with gorse in Co. Armagh. The horsemen pursued and followed up his track so closely that they were able to dismount, and with sword in hand searched the hillside where he lay in ambush, and at one time a sword was plunged into the gorse within a short distance of where he lay. But as it was getting dark, they mounted their horses and rode off in the direction of Newry, and . . . tired and hungry he made his way back to his home.[11]

John Brontë calls his family 'a peculiar family . . . quite different from the ordinary folk in intellectual grasp'. His evidence is that the Brontë brothers of Patrick's generation were unsuperstitious, though other witnesses are found to say the contrary. He instances an occasion when James Brontë refuted a story of fairies playing and singing in an old 'forth' by saying 'Fairies Hell! There's no such thing as fairies. All lies and superstition!' John Brontë also tells of an occasion when the Brontë brothers in their capacity as roadmen took on the completion of a road through a 'forth', after a previous contractor had died on the job and it had been supposed this was due to supernatural agency.

According to John Brontë links between Haworth and Ireland remained strong. He calls the view that Patrick cut himself off from his family 'lying trash' and tells of the stir caused by Charlotte's death. His own father's name was Patrick, and he claims this was in honour of the clergyman of Haworth. He has two letters written by Patrick in his possession, written to Hugh and Mary Brontë respectively, in 1855 and 1859. These letters, printed most recently in *The Brontës of Ballynaskeagh*, will be referred to later.

It might be said that John Brontë's position here is that the Irish Brontës were respectable and above the superstitious nonsense of their neighbours. He lays emphasis on the connections with Haworth and quotes the letters to show that Patrick retained an interest in family welfare into his final decade. As a successful man himself, he sees the Ballynahinch affair through romantic spectacles, stressing the daring while playing down the rebellious aspect. His attitude does not seem far from that of Patrick himself, seeing Ireland as a place to be left behind, but anxious to emphasise both the wild aspect of derring-do and the contradictory respectability of a family on the edge of the bourgeoisie.

Rose Heslip and Maggie Shannon exhibit similar ambivalence. They are both anxious to claim a part in the respectable story of the bestselling author, which requires them to divulge details of the family past; but both shy away from the close scrutiny of the more distant prospects of that past, and in any case lack positive information with which to counteract the Hugh Brunty legend as told by Wright. Both were undoubtedly the recipients of considerable attention because of their slight connection with Charlotte, and Rose Heslip, living as she did in Yorkshire, was the better able to take her share of the limelight. Her picture featured in the *Brontë Society Transactions* and the Society sent a representative to her funeral.

Maggie Shannon was the granddaughter of Welsh or Walsh Brontë, Patrick's brother, and thus was Patrick's great-niece. For McKay she played down Brontë eccentricities, while for Wright she played them up. She confirmed the origin of Hugh Brunty as Drogheda, and added that he

> was an only son and had just one sister, and they were living with an uncle, a brother of their mother's, in Drogheda, both parents being dead.[12]

This does not square with Alice's account, quoted previously. Whereas Alice (who was of an older generation than Maggie Shannon) recalled the adoption of Hugh at the age of eight, Maggie makes the assumption that both his natural parents were dead. Alice accords better with Wright in ascribing the 'sister' to 'Welsh' and Hugh's aunt, so that she would be Hugh's cousin. Maggie then adds a piece of the jigsaw not otherwise found in mentioning Hilltown as a place where Hugh lived between leaving Drogheda and arriving at Ballynaskeagh: 'Hugh afterwards came down to the neighbourhood of Hilltown to some relatives of his mother.'[13] We may note that neither informant states positively that the uncle in Drogheda was called Brunty; he may perfectly well have been known as Welsh or Walsh.

Wright quotes Maggie Shannon in *The Bookman* of December 1896 as corroborating in a vague way the fact that Hugh Brontë, Patrick's brother, had visited England.[14] There he had seen the Queen in London and visited the home of Sir John Armitage, where he had tried on Robin Hood's helmet. He was given a silver pencil-case by Patrick, who had sent one to each brother in Ireland, and a silver thimble to each sister.

To McKay, Maggie sternly said, 'There was nothing remarkable about [the Brontës] more than any other family save their foreign appearance and quickness to resent insults', an account not totally reassuring.[15] To Wright, meanwhile, she wrote of 'the mischief-loving Brontës', giving two examples. The first concerned a practical joke, in which the Brontë brothers went out at night and by using 'flint and steel and a bit of tinder' they made the furze bushes seem to be on fire. This episode, in Caldwell's Fields, culminated in the surprise of the locals in the morning when they discovered that their furze was not burnt and that the whole thing had been an illusion. 'These, and many another trick, it was their delight to play on their unsuspecting neighbours,' says Maggie Shannon, 'and when old, they lived their youth over again, as they recounted them to their neighbours.' Once again we encounter the Brontës' talent for oral story-telling.

The second incident related by Maggie concerned James Brontë. He is alleged to have dressed up as a fortune-teller, borrowing skirts, cap, bonnet and other female garb from his sister and going round the neighbours unrecognised to tell them their fortunes. They 'thinking he was a real gipsy', paid him with flax, honey, meal and money, which he returned a few days later when he told them of the trick. Wright comments that the groundwork of the gypsy fortune-teller episode in *Jane Eyre* may have its origins in this. To know whether this could be so, we should need to know when the fortune-telling trick was played by James; certainly the possibility cannot be ruled out, and at a later stage I shall consider whether James may have visited Haworth about the time *Jane Eyre* was being contemplated and written.

Rose Heslip was even more loquacious than Maggie Shannon, and more accessible. She was born in 1821, the daughter of Simon Collins and Sarah Brunty. She had lived in Ballynaskeagh until about 1838, during which time she had worked for her uncle Hugh. She told Horsfall Turner that Sarah Brunty had run away with Simon Collins and that the wedding had been at a register office; in 1806 or thereabouts this seems unlikely. Among many pieces of information about the Brontë family which she gave to Wright, McKay, Ramsden and Turner, the following points seem most important.

Rose remembered that her uncle Hugh had been to England while she was working for him.[16] This must have been between about 1827 and 1837, but perhaps more probably towards the end of this period. As we have seen, Maggie Shannon told the same story, and said that he had been in London and Yorkshire, and had been given a silver pencil-case. Unfortunately in *The Sketch*, Rose Heslip threw doubt on the date of the visit by claiming it was when Hugh was 'a boy'.[17] Patrick was not in Yorkshire before 1811, by which time Hugh was thirty. Nor could Rose herself have remembered the visit if he had gone there when a boy, since she wasn't born until 1821. She did, however, add reasons for Hugh's visit; he had gone to help in corn-thrashing, and had been shown Robin Hood's grave. Migrations of Irish farm-workers to help with the harvest were of course a seasonal feature of the English landscape at the time.[18] Rose confirmed that James too had visited Yorkshire, and in fact he had been to Haworth.

Transcripts of two letters of Wright to Mrs Heslip are preserved at Haworth.[19] In them he replies to allegations that he had not told the truth in *The Brontës in Ireland*. It appears that Rose may have been taking him to task for making the Brontës appear uncouth, for he agrees he has toned down the account of the fight between Welsh and Sam Clarke. This admission is not encouraging in considering the total veracity of Wright, but it does make it seem possible that his editing would be in the direction of making some aspects of the nineteenth-century Brontës appear less sensational than they were, rather than more so.

Matters between Rose Heslip and Wright came to a head in *The Sketch* for February and March 1897. Described there as a lady of 'intellectual force', Rose denied the story of Welsh the foundling outright, giving however the rather curious reason for her denial that 'My Uncle Welsh was a constant visitor, but I never heard it once named among them', as though she thought her uncle Welsh was the Welsh referred to in the story, when the Welsh in question was of two generations previous.[20] The shadowy 'sister' of Hugh, 'Aunt Mary', had indeed paid a visit from the neighbourhood of Drogheda; old Alice (not Patrick's sister, but his mother Eilís) had been fair-haired. Hugh and James had been road-contractors, and James had been a shoemaker, but could turn his hand to anything. Her uncle Hugh had not died, as Wright said, after an encounter with a ghost, but lived to be an old man; James's visit to Haworth was well remembered, and he had reported Charlotte as 'very inquisitive . . . wanted a heap of news'. She had a 'very wee foot and was dim of sight, though her eyes were sharp and clear'.

Wright took issue with some of the details of Rose's interview with *The Sketch*, and once again reiterated the story of Patrick's 'frequent' visits to Ballynaskeagh. He told *Sketch* readers that he and Mrs Heslip had disagreed over an incident he had recorded, in which her uncle Hugh had 'disposed of' Mr McKee's tea while waiting for the verdict on *Jane Eyre*. She had said, 'Och, man, sure yon's not the kind o' thing to put in a book.'[21] The comment may be revealing about the manner in which Rose Heslip (and perhaps Maggie Shannon and others) edited the information they gave to Wright, McKay and Ramsden. More justifiably, perhaps, Rose Heslip disliked the 'magpie's blood' episode given in *The Brontës in Ireland* (pp. 284–5), in which Hugh is supposed to have fashioned a shillelagh and dipped it in blood when on the track of the *Quarterly* reviewer. 'Shure, it makes him look like a haythen', Rose is alleged to have told Wright. However, she does not seem to have denied the episode was true, only claimed it was discreditable. If it was of such relatives that Charlotte heard when her father talked to her about Ireland, can we be surprised at her recoil?

The controversy in *The Academy* with Andrew Lang brought no new witnesses, but it did call forth a supplementary point from Wright who had written in his book of the 'tragic death' of Welsh, the wicked uncle. He now said that the death had taken place one night when the uncle had come home drunk and driven his wife, Mary, out of the house. He had evidently fallen on the fire, since in the morning his body was found burnt to death. Unfortunately Wright gives no date nor source for this story and it is presumably one of the events that he admits to suppressing in his introduction.[22]

5 Origins: the Brontës in the Seventeenth and Eighteenth Centuries

In these first four chapters we have tried to clear the evidential ground a little. We have examined our main witness, William Wright, discussing his merits and failings as a historian; we have looked at the characters and capacities of his informants; we have introduced a series of would-be Brontë chroniclers such as Ramsden, Horsfall Turner and McKay; and we have listed the various Brontë descendants whose memories were called upon in the 1890s to support or demolish Wright's story. We have seen that the Brontë Society establishment, led by Shorter, muzzled these wild Irish rumours and banished Wright, so that he does not even merit an obituary in the *Brontë Society Transactions*. This leaves Charlotte the respectable English bourgeoise, and confirms Patrick in his attempts to seal up for ever the buried cache of his own past and that of his relations in Ireland. Wright half-dragged the buried material to the surface; the Brontë Society establishment pushed it back and piled soil on it.

But if the nineteenth-century history of the Brontës in Ireland is difficult to unearth, their history prior to that is even more so. When we come to consider exactly what old Hugh Brunty told his neighbours as he sat by the fire and beeked the corn, and whether he told truth or legend, we are necessarily concerned with the balance of probabilities rather than precise historical knowledge. We must still rely on Wright and his informants. Records and documents will be less available, but we must make the best we can of them.

In one sense, the main thesis of this book, that the Brontës at Haworth were conscious of an Irish dimension and that this found its way into their writings, is not affected by the truth or falsehood of what they heard. If any legendary material from

Ireland, felt by Emily to be family history, reached *Wuthering Heights* or the poems, or if any of Charlotte's obsession with the orphan child can be traced to stories told by Hugh Brunty, this is almost good enough. Not quite, however, since I shall suggest that the intensity of *Wuthering Heights* may in part result from the feeling that family history, the repetition of characteristics, the vengeful influence of the outcast from the family, are all matters of personal interest to Emily. In Geraldine and Iernë she produces two Gondal self-identifications with an Irish flavour. In *Wuthering Heights* she tells of a family feud and near-disaster in a manner reminiscent of hero-legend and ballad. Weighing the possibility that there was objective truth behind any impression she may have had that she was herself part of such a legend cannot entirely be evaded.

Let us return to our first published Brontë biographical source, Mrs Gaskell. In 1857 she wrote,

> The Rev. Patrick Brontë is a native of the County Down in Ireland. His father, Hugh Brontë, was left an orphan at an early age. He came from the south to the north of the island, and settled in the parish of Aghaderg, near Loughbrickland. There was some family tradition that, humble as Hugh Brontë's circumstances were, he was the descendant of an ancient family.[1]

Mrs Gaskell seems to have based this account on a letter written by Patrick on 20 June 1855 in which he says,

> My father's name was Hugh Brontë. He was a native of the south of Ireland, and was left an orphan at an early age. It was said he was of ancient family. Whether this was or was not so I never gave myself the trouble to inquire, since his lot in life depended, under Providence, not on family descent but our own exertions. He came to the north of Ireland, and made an early but suitable marriage. His pecuniary means were small – but, renting a few acres of land, he and my mother by dint of application and industry managed to bring up a family of ten children, in a respectable manner. I shew'd an early fondness for books, and continued at school for several years. At the age of sixteen – knowing that my father could afford me no pecuniary aid – I began to think of doing something for

myself. I therefore opened a public school – in this line I continued for six years. I was then a tutor in a gentleman's family – from which situation I removed to Cambridge and entered St. John's College.[2]

This letter will be referred to later. It was not, of course, available to Wright, Ramsden, McKay, or any of the early commentators on the Brontës in Ireland.

It seems likely that the extract from Mrs Gaskell's biography was a stimulus to Wright in his investigations. Both Patrick Brontë and Mrs Gaskell use phrases suggesting that Hugh Brunty had a southern origin and 'came to the North'. As we have seen and shall discuss further, younger members of the Brontë family knew that his origin was near Drogheda, and we may assume that Patrick, the eldest, also knew this but did not choose to reveal it. 'The south' may seem more romantic than Drogheda, and both Charlotte and Patrick are later found writing of Killarney. It is possible that Patrick's location of his father's origin in 'the south of Ireland' may be a hint of a Catholic and Gælic background which Patrick may be trying to account for.

The effect of Mrs Gaskell's story on Wright seems to have been to make him set off to explore the south of Ireland, and during his expedition he passed through the Boyne valley. His misunderstanding of Mrs Gaskell and Patrick Brontë, who perhaps knew little about his father before he came to the Boyne, sent Wright looking in the south for Hugh's own birthplace. One or two straws in the wind suggest that he was looking in the wrong place once he had gone south of the Boyne. Before we can understand why this is so, we must examine some elements in eighteenth-century Irish demography. By doing so, we should be able to establish the distribution of the Brunty/Pronty surname.

Though many Irish records were destroyed in the fire at the Four Courts in Dublin, the situation is by no means one of desperation. It is possible, using Hearth Money rolls from the seventeenth century and the Tithe Applotment and Griffith's survey lists from the nineteenth to get some idea of the distribution of surnames in the intervening period. The nineteenth-century lists show versions of the Brontë surname that are near the Irish (Ó Pronntaigh) clustering in a band from south-west of Belturbet and Cavan to north-west of Armagh city. The incidence of Prunty and Pronty is greatest at the west end of this corridor, around Newtownbutler to Monaghan (nineteen families), though there are scattered incidences to the south west, in Roscommon and Longford, where the name tends towards Printy or Prenty. To the east, in County Down, as we know, it becomes Brunty and Bronty. It would seem most sensible to seek the origin of the name where it is both commonest and nearest its Irish form.

Edward MacLysaght in *More Irish Families* traces the name in County Monaghan (O'Prounty) and Armagh (O'Prunty), both on Hearth Money rolls.[3] He finds no (O') Pruntys south of Drogheda. There are no Pruntys or Prontys south of the Boyne in the nineteenth-century lists except for one isolated example in Carlow. The Armagh local historian T. G. F. Paterson traces the occurrence of the name during the seventeenth and eighteenth centuries.[4] His findings support MacLysaght. He finds the first record of a Prunty in Armagh manor in 1625, where Hugh O Prunty appears on a court roll on 11 October. Donell O Prenty appears as a witness at Hockley, Armagh, in 1641–2, and Paterson records Thomas O Pronty in Armagh manor in 1664. Also on the Hearth Money rolls for the year are Teage O Pronty and Edmund O Pronty, appearing for Lurghaboy, Barony of Orrier. Torlagh Bronty was a tenant of Armagh manor in 1714, among a list of Catholic tenants. We need also to make a first mention here of an Irish poet, Pádraig Ó Pronntaigh, whom Douglas Hyde believed to have been a forebear of Patrick, and to whom we must return.

Paterson also noted Pruntys in Tyrone. He finds one in Dungannon in the 1666 Hearth Money rolls, who turns out to be one Owen O'Pronty of Killimuil. He seems likely to have been the ancestor of a second Edmund Prunty, who one hundred years later, in 1766, occurs in a householders' list for Drumglass (Dungannon). Quite surprisingly, Paterson finds that John and William Bronte (so spelt) were tenants in 1780 of Henry Stafford Willock at Tullyquilly, Rathfriland, not more than three miles from Imdel. The occurrence of such a spelling in the late eighteenth century may help us to understand why Wright insisted that the name had always been Brontë, despite the evidence of Drumballyroney church registers. Finally, Paterson confirms MacLysaght's record of O'Prountys in Monaghan with Patrick and Philip of Carrickanare, Tullycorbet, in 1663.

We may conclude that the name O'Prunty, and its variants, is found in a cluster centred on a corridor from Newtownbutler to Armagh, with offshoots, whose names become progressively less like Ó Pronntaigh, further west and east. There is almost no trace on paper of the name south of the Boyne, and it is no wonder that Wright could find none when he dressed up as a peasant and went in search of Brontës about 1858. We need to bear this distribution in mind when we are trying to trace the origin of Hugh Brunty.

First, however, we shall look at Wright's account again. We recall that by 1858 he had three clues to the location of the 'Brontë' farm, as he would consider it to be. He had the versions of Hugh's own story which he had heard in infancy and revised with William McAlister; he had the tradition known to the surviving members of the family that Hugh had come from near Drogheda; and he now had Mrs Gaskell's short account, which was rather misleading. We shall first consider what he made of these clues, then see whether there are further data which Wright did not know about.

We can find two slightly different layers of writing in *The Brontës in Ireland* about this topic. On page 49 Wright says that the Brunty farm was 'on the north side of the River Boyne, between Oldbridge and Navan', and on page 74 adds that it was 'near the spot where a wing of William's army crossed the Boyne on that era-making day in 1690'. Lower down page 49 he says the ruins were actually 'pointed out' to him. On the face of it, this modifies his original information that the farm was between Oldbridge and Navan, and suggests that this vaguer location may represent an earlier version told to him by informants in County Down. We can discover quite easily where Wright's ruins were, though typically he does not pinpoint them on a map for us. The right wing of William's army crossed the Boyne near Rosnaree ford, perhaps a little below the ford itself since the summer of 1690 was dry and the river running low. If Wright is accurate, the Brunty house was on the opposite side from Rosnaree, in Monknewtown parish, and we must search for it within a mile or so of the ford.

Were Wright's ruins really the ruins of the Brunty farm? We can accept that he was shown a ruined house near Oldbridge in 1858, which he was given to understand was once the home of Hugh Brunty. In a little while we shall move forward to try to identify this pile of ruins on a large-scale map. But there is a loophole, so that we must say that any ruins we so identify can only be one alternative identification of Hugh Brunty's early home. For it is quite possible that Wright misunderstood information given to him in 1858, or that his informant misunderstood his question.

As it happens, a year or two later another enquirer walked along the Boyne valley seeking information and was given an answer to his question that satisfied him. About 1860 the Revd James O'Laverty came to Monknewtown seeking proof that the ancient barrows in the area (which we shall be examining ourselves shortly) were really the burial sites of the old Irish kings.[5] The ancient kings had been buried at a place called Brugh na Boinne. O'Laverty wanted to know if there were any place names still in existence which might confirm the name. He was 'greatly pleased' when Mr Maguire of New Grange told him that the field in which New Grange mound is situated was called the *Bro-park* 'while in the immediate vicinity are the *Bro-Farm*, the *Bro-Mill* and the *Bro-Cottage*'. The similarity between these names and the name Brontë cannot be glossed over. Is it possible that Mr Maguire (a local farmer who can be identified from the *Parish Valuation of Ireland*) may have been accustomed to dealing with people who came asking about the location of a house connected with a name beginning Bro-, and customarily told them that they had found the right place, then showed them a pile of ruins? There is absolutely no way of answering this query, and I shall leave the matter open for a time, while we examine the terrain.

Whether or not Wright's ruins actually were Hugh Brunty's old home, it was certainly within sight of the prehistoric tumuli at Brugh na Boinne. It is a haunted countryside. To Wright, the Ulster Presbyterian, the Boyne valley just here was redolent with the stirring history of the late seventeenth century: no one in Northern Ireland could forget the significance of the spot where in that decisive and ever-commemorated victory the Protestant succession was secured. But the 'bend in the Boyne', as I have hinted, was already a place abounding in archæological and historical significance centuries before William of Orange had been thought of. An area steeped in the memories of ancient bloodshed, it had been the centre for the reverence of Irishmen and for the telling of miraculous tales of folk-lore since prehistoric times. The great tumulus at New Grange, first excavated scientifically in 1890, is now thought to have been the burial place of the ancient kings of Tara; there are other great tumuli at Dowth and Knowth, and legends have circulated round them since time immemorial. Some examples of the nature of these legends will be given shortly.[6]

New Grange tumulus is the largest of the three great tumuli in the area. It was explored in 1699 and was noted by several antiquaries of the time, who describe its hollow burial-chamber as a 'cave'. Literary evidence from the Irish hero-cycles provides the link with the ancient King Aengus, a part-supernatural figure about whom stories of great deeds gathered. The entrance to the burial-chamber was and is by means of a small shaft, with a trilithon as its gateway and a mysterious marked stone partly blocking the path. Like many other ancient sites of this character, the mound has been linked by some archæologists with prehistoric sun-worship.

This mound and its neighbours came to be considered by the people of the Boyne valley as the home of the Tuatha de Danaan, the race of conquering kings who dwindled in stature down the ages until they became the fairies, entering and leaving their 'raths' in columns by moonlight. When W. Y. Evans-Wentz was collecting material for his *The Fairy Faith in Celtic Countries* in 1908–10 he visited New Grange and at once met informants who could tell him a great deal about the 'good people' in the area. Mr Owen Morgan of Rosnaree gave him the tale of the shoemaker's daughter who became the Queen of Tara. The tale begins with three children stolen by fairies and in each case a little 'leprechaun' left in its place.[7] One should not be too influenced in visualising these creatures by children's stories of the twentieth century. There was something more than a little sinister about these otherworld beings, with their crumpled or cross-eyed faces and their irrationality; Heathcliff has more than a touch of changeling in him. Thus the existence in popular story of goblin-like substitute children is clearly attested in the countryside where Hugh Brunty grew up.

Next Evans-Wentz talked to Maggie Timmons, a milkmaid. She assured him that 'the good people' used to be seen coming in and out of the 'fort' at New Grange at morning and evening.[8] When asked what the good people were like, Maggie replied that when they disappeared they went like fog. 'They must be something like spirits, or how could they disappear in that way? I knew of people . . . who would milk in the fields about here and spill milk on the ground for the *good people*; and pots of potatoes would be put out for the *good people* at night.' Later, Uncle James Brontë was to state that he disbelieved in fairies, while his niece Emily enjoyed making up lengthy and beguiling stories about them in her childhood.

It should not be too difficult to decide where Wright's pile of ruins was. The Boyne is bordered on the north by the civil parish of Monknewtown, with its ruined church at some distance from the river. The three riverside townlands are, from west to east, Crewbane, Knowth and New Grange. The last faces Rosnaree directly. To the west lies Slane, with its large estate and castle. Next to the east, still lying within Wright's limits 'from Oldbridge to Navan', is the parish of Dowth. Behind this lies Townley Hall, owned by the Marquis of Drogheda, with its planted parks, walks, orchards and purlieus. This terrain accords well with what Wright says of the country held out to Hugh as a bait by his uncle Welsh, as he pleaded with him to leave his parents and come to the Boyne valley. What we cannot know is whether this was in Hugh's original account, or whether Wright added it when he had travelled along the Boyne (see Map 2).

Wright's ruins cannot have been in Slane. It cannot really be said to be 'near the spot' where William's army crossed. As we read through the account in *The Brontës in Ireland* we obtain a picture of a farm rather than a smallholding, with herds of cattle, but also a field of oats 'in a remote corner of the farm' (p. 73). There is also some bogland, disputed with a neighbour (pp. 67–8) and at least one 'lone plantation' in the neighbourhood, where a repellant character named Gallagher, with an accomplice, Meg, helped Welsh to engineer his alleged marriage to Mary Brunty, Hugh's aunt (pp. 29, 53). The neighbour with whom Welsh has the argument over the piece of bogland becomes a friend to Hugh and helps him to escape by swimming *downstream* from his uncle's holding to a point opposite a clump of willows, where the neighbour waits with clothes in which Hugh can make his departure (p. 74).

If we examine nineteenth-century records of Monknewtown we find on the Ordnance Survey plans a number of houses marked on early editions which had gone by the later versions.

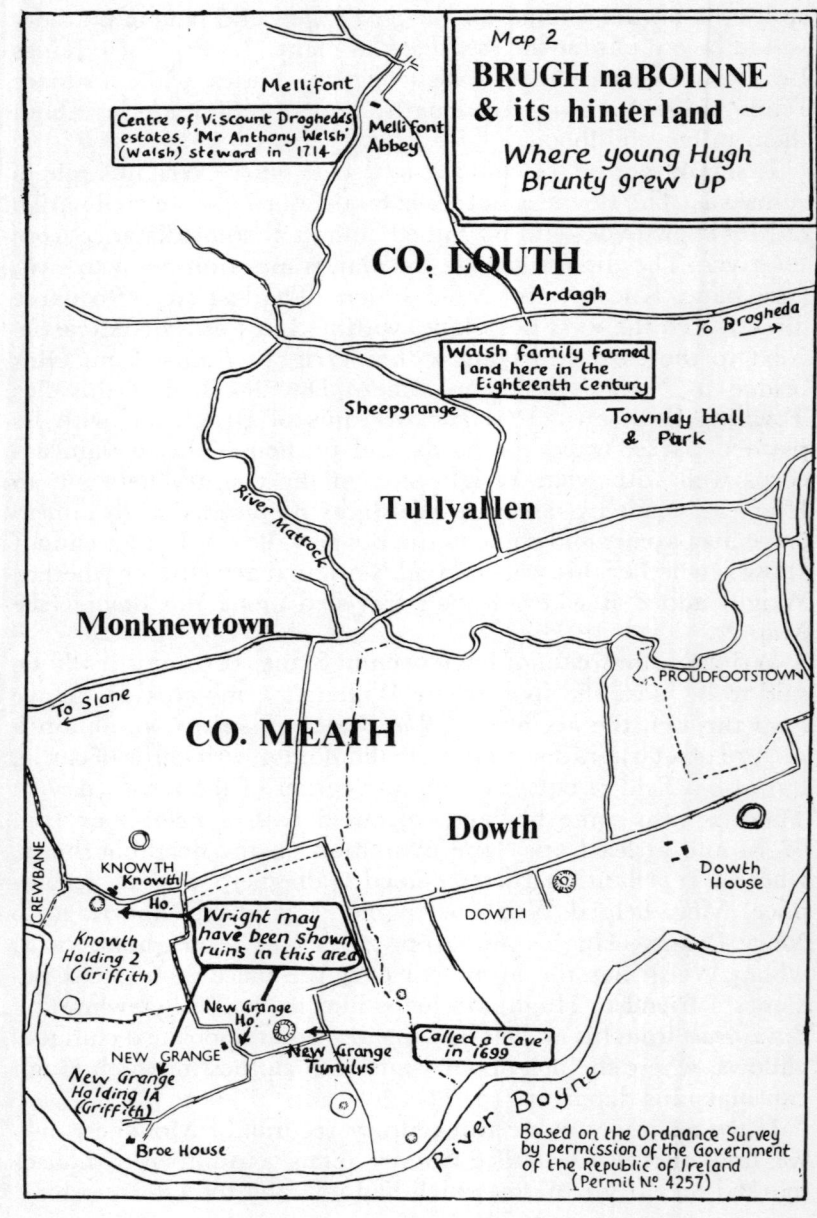

In Crewbane there are no farmhouses, though two 'herdsmen's houses' are shown in *Parish Valuation of Ireland*. At Knowth we find that there were nine houses recorded on the 1841 census, falling to eight in 1851, after the potato famine. Wright suggests (pp. 49–50) that the famine may have been the cause of the disappearance of the Brontë house. In New Grange houses fall from twenty to thirteen during the 1840s, and the population goes down from 138 in 1841 to 65 in 1861, three years after Wright was shown the ruins of the house.

The Parish Valuation gives the names of two Gallaghers, one at Slane town, one near the edge of Crewbane. This does not prove Hugh Brunty's story, but it is interesting to find the name represented in the locality. Crewbane itself seems too far west to allow Hugh to have swum to the ford. Both Knowth (holding 2 in *The Parish Valuation*) and New Grange (holding 1a) were in the ownership of the Maguire family in the 1840s. We can see on the 1837 first edition OS 6-inch map a fairly extensive building at the back of the great tumulus at Knowth which had disappeared by the time of the next edition. This may have been the Brontë house as shown to Wright in 1858. Here Welsh may have dwelt, on land which the Bruntys had laboured to reclaim and build into a fine cattle farm.

However, it ought to be said that no extant plan or document from the eighteenth century mentions the name of Brontë or Prunty, or anything like it, on land near New Grange. A land map for the Caldwell estates in Knowth and New Grange dated 1766 gives no such name, and the Earl of Sheffield's tax lists for 1798 are equally unhelpful.[9] While it is quite possible that the Bruntys or Welsh could have been sub-tenants whose names might not appear on maps, the result of these searches is certainly discouraging. We cannot doubt Wright's location for what he thought was the Brontë farm, but nothing on any document bears out his story, apart from the name of Gallagher.

But when we cast the net a little wider we uncover a strange group of coincidences which may after all allow us to think that there was something in the story Wright had heard from his informants about the unhappy life of Hugh Brunty. As we shall see in the following chapter there was in the very near neighbourhood of New Grange a family called Walsh, and that this Walsh was a steward (or as Wright calls it 'agent'), and that there was violence in the parish of Dowth against one of the

Walsh family. All this will take us back to the generations before Hugh Brunty himself. For the moment we have discovered the approximate place where Hugh Brunty grew up after the age of eight, and have described it as one of the most extraordinary places in Ireland, rich in mysterious legend and remote history.

It is not to be thought that the Brontë sisters, or even Patrick Brontë, realised the full significance of this place where Hugh had lived. Though the daughters may have read Moore's *History of Ireland* (this is quite likely in view of their general interest in his work, though we have no positive evidence of it) they are unlikely to have been aware that his reference (p. 44) to 'the great barrow at New Grange' could have had a personal significance for them. In considering exactly what Patrick Brontë told them about their forebears, we cannot be sure how far he knew the precise location of the Brunty farm in the Boyne valley. He is quite certain to have known that the farm was 'near Drogheda', but he had never been there, nor asked (according to his own word in the letter to Mrs Gaskell) much about the farm. It must be stressed again that to Ulster Protestants the term 'Battle of the Boyne' had nothing to do with the heroic deeds of the old kings of Tara.

But though Patrick Brontë and his daughters consciously and continuously emphasised the Scots element in their Ulster heritage, in their own case at least such an element may have been fictional. South Down is not very Scottish. At the 1659 'census' there were no Scots in Glascar or Ballynaskeagh and no English. When we look later on at the travels of the Ordnance Surveyor, we shall see that the area round Rathfriland and Castlewellan was called by then the 'Irish' district. If the Brontës acquired their well-known attachment to Scotland and the Scots landscape and tradition under the impression that it was their own heritage, they were wrong. It is unlikely that Patrick Brontë could pretend to himself that he was somehow Scots, but one or two circumstances may have helped the children to think so.

For example, Hugh Brunty is said to have spoken with a 'distinctly Scottish' accent.[10] Wright's informant in this matter was W. J. McCracken, presumably relying in part on the impression of his mother, Patrick's pupil, Elizabeth Wilson. This accent was also noted by a *Banbridge Chronicle* reporter.[11] Mrs Gaskell wrote of Patrick after her first meeting with him that he spoke 'with a strong Scotch accent (he comes from the North of

Ireland)'.¹² Despite Mary Taylor's comment that Charlotte spoke with an Irish accent, this Scots flavour is thus evidenced three times, and requires investigation.¹³

The real problem is to try to guess what these commentators individually identified as a Scots sound. A certain precision perhaps, clear pronunciation of the letter 'r', lengthening of vowels in general, and perhaps a thinness about the 'u' sound. The *Banbridge Chronicle* writer, contributing the obituary of Alice Brontë says that,

> Her very accent was so different from the present vulgar tongue of the locality. . . . It had that decided Scottish flavour for which the inhabitants were formerly remarkable.

This writer would have been well versed in different Ulster intonations. What he may have been hearing was first generation English, replacing Irish and carrying some of the sound values of that language more obviously than the second generation, less carefully articulated, speech which replaced it. But if Hugh, Patrick or Alice had sounded *Southern* Irish, McCracken's informant, Mrs Gaskell, or the *Banbridge Chronicle* journalist would have noticed this.

To expand this point: if Hugh Brunty's birthplace had been Killarney, for example, and he had spoken the English of the South, this would not have been mistaken by anyone for Scots. The English spoken in the South of Ireland had originated in the West of England. It was the ancestor of the 'stage' Irish of the nineteenth century. This kind of speech was separated from the speech of Ulster by a broad bank of native Irish stretching through Louth, Armagh and South Down. As Wright began belatedly to think, it was unlikely that Hugh Brunty could have learned his English to the south of that area. Wright does not consider at all the question of what language Hugh Brunty spoke in childhood. We shall look into the matter at a later stage and proffer the view that Hugh's mother tongue may not have been English at all.

It is time now to return to the matter of that birthplace and to consider Wright's account of the journey by which Hugh was removed from his parental home to an exile in the Boyne valley. Wright had thought this home was in the South. On page 49, he admits very candidly 'It is quite possible I may have been on the wrong track.... His journey, after all, may have been from the north', and he quotes the evidence of the Scots accent, as mentioned above. It is too late now to dress up in peasants' clothing and wander the lanes of the North in search of Bruntys. We have to make the best we can of Wright's description of the long miserable journey of Hugh, Welsh and Mary.

Wright gives a great deal of detail about the journey, appearing to regard it as very important. The story was first told to him 'by my old tutor, the Rev. William McAllister, and confirmed subsequently by several of his friends who were men of intelligence and education.... By four independent narrators the account was repeated to me.'[14] Details had differed slightly, but not much. Some striking incidents had been omitted by Wright, as they had not appeared in all four accounts. We must be sorry for this, since one of them may have given a clue which Wright had not noticed.

It is probably pointless to guess who were the four narrators Wright listened to. They would be people with whom he was on good terms in the 1850s. McKee might be one of them; McAlister was another. Beyond that we cannot go, and there is thus no way of testing the veracity of the informants. All that can be said is that Hugh's story of his journey into exile was memorable, and that it fits the theory that his home was in the North at least as well as the opposite.

The following is the bare outline of Hugh's story. He had been living in a comfortable home with his brothers and sisters. His father was a man in prosperous circumstances.[15]

Strangers arrived, claiming to be Hugh's aunt and uncle. The uncle's name was Welsh, and he had a dark face and dark hair. The pair promised Hugh a life of luxury if he would come with them, and he agreed. He was fitted out with a new suit of clothes, and one evening the aunt and uncle took leave of the family, placing Hugh in a cart and setting out on a long journey to the Boyne valley.[16]

Hardly had they left the family home when the uncle's attitude changed completely. Instead of being kind to little Hugh (whose precise age is not given by the oral tradition) Welsh became abusive and cruel. The journey became a nightmare instead of a pleasure. An argument arose about money, and it became clear that the motive for adopting Hugh was financial. The sum of £50 per annum is mentioned.[17]

The route is described in some detail. On the first night Hugh watched the watery moon and stars, suffering 'utter desolation' in his feeling of rejection.

> When he awoke it was broad day. . . . After a while he sat up in the straw and looked over the sides of the cart. He was in a strange and unknown land. On the west rose a mountain abloom with heather. The rising sun shone upon it, and gave a golden tint to the ruby heath. On the east, bordered by the sea, stretched a level plain composed of barren bog and rocky scrubland.[18]

At a later stage Wright suggests that the 'sea' could have been a large lake.

This land was desolate and the track on which the cart was jogging 'could hardly be called a road'. Hugh fell asleep, but when he woke up the cart had stopped and the sun was beating down on his face. They were near a thatched cottage which comprised both a grocer's shop and a public house. A blacksmith who was working nearby helped Hugh down from the cart. At this point his aunt appeared and led him 'gently' into the cottage, where he slept until the afternoon.[19] He was not permitted to talk to the inhabitants. Before they set out again, he was allowed to spend the few pennies he had been given by his brothers and sisters. 'It was ten years before I fingered another penny that I could call my own', he said later.

The second night's journey was through drizzling rain. The horse splashed through mud the whole night, sometimes walking and sometimes at a trot. About ten o'clock the next morning a large village was reached. In later years Hugh could not identify it. Thus ended the second night's journey.

The large village had an inn 'of considerable importance'. Hugh was put to bed, but no one except his aunt came near him. She took away his clothes and later substituted a suit of bottle-green corduroy much too large for him. Hugh told later of his hatred for these clothes.[20] That night, their third, the journey was continued, but nothing is said about it. Another large town was reached in the morning and the cart was drawn up at the local inn.

During the day the uncle went about some business and Hugh stole to the innkeeper and tried to tell him of his plight. Wright says 'the man could not comprehend what he said, and he could not understand what the man said owing to the brogue'. A crowd gathered, and Hugh was 'just beginning to make himself understood when the uncle returned suddenly and whisked him off to the cart, where he was obliged to spend the long afternoon'. On reflection, we may think that it was not merely 'the brogue' which was the problem, but that little Hugh was talking Irish. On a later occasion, after the 1798 rebellion, this is said by Wright to have been an advantage; in or about 1760, during this present encounter, Hugh could not make himself understood.

Of the fourth night nothing is said except that it was 'miserable', and so on the morning of the fourth day of travel, they arrived at Drogheda.[21] There was a short pause, after which the cart started again, and they all reached the banks of the Boyne in the late afternoon.

It will be realised that the above is a summary of Wright's summaries. There is some vagueness, but a number of points are quite clear: that the adoption was for payment; that it was against Hugh's will and the aunt and uncle kept him away from outside influence; that there were four nights on the journey and that Drogheda was reached before proceeding to the Boyne farm.

On the basis of this story Wright toured Southern Ireland in peasant garb. He found nothing south of the Boyne. As has been said, he later begins to think he was looking in the wrong direction and changes his view. The journey was from the north, not the south. There are many reasons why we may well agree with Wright's later view. Let us take the evidence and examine it piece by piece.

The fourth night of the journey ended with the arrival of the cart in Drogheda. Had Hugh's aunt and uncle been travelling from the south-west, this could not have happened. Had they been travelling along a coastal road from the south, they would have passed through Dublin, which Hugh could not have failed to mention. To the east of Drogheda is the Irish Sea. Hugh had not come, then, from a wide arc from west to east. He could only have come from a direction either north or north West.

There are three straws in the wind tending to support this view. First, the Scottish accent. This may or may not be significant, since the *Banbridge Chronicle* suggests that other natives of Ballynaskeagh used to speak in this way. Unfortunately we do not know what is meant by 'Scottish'. Second, a rather odd point concerned with corn-beeking. In *Folk Life*, vol. 2, Dr Alan Gailey refers to Wright's account of the Brontë kiln in order to describe a folklore theory concerned with the prevalent geographical drift of Ulster culture.[22] The Brontë kiln, it seems, was unique. All other corn-kilns traced by Dr Gailey were to the north-west of Ulster, in a distribution stretching in an arc from Donegal through Londonderry and fading out some miles west of Lough Neagh. It must be regarded as a possibility that Hugh Brunty had turned to this method of earning his living after seeing this kind of corn-kiln in operation in this north-western area: it seems unlikely that he would be able to copy the idea of corn-beeking from local or southern exemplars.

The third particle of evidence which needs to be taken into account is the remark of Maggie Shannon to McKay that Hugh first arrived at 'the neighbourhood of Hilltown' when he ran away from the Boyne farm, and, very interestingly, 'to some relatives of his mother'.[23] If Hugh Brunty's mother had connections in Hilltown, four or five miles south of Rathfriland, this may be an added reason for suspecting a northern, rather than southern, place of birth. Much later, Patrick Brontë writes of Killarney, and possibly liked to believe that his origins lay in such a romantic spot. Whether Hugh himself had any idea at all where he had originated, we do not know. Wright lays stress on his ignorance and suggests that this was contrived on purpose by his aunt and uncle. I shall mention later the probability that Hugh may have felt some connection with the area round Dundalk.

Like Wright, we may wish to try to work out where this night journey led. We have one advantage: we are not tied to the theory that it led from the south. Unless Wright is at fault, we know that on an August morning one year about 1760, Hugh Brunty aged between six and eight, arrived in a cart with his aunt and adopted uncle at Drogheda, and that by the afternoon they had come home to a place near New Grange. Wright calculates on page 48 that the speed of the cart would be about 2 1/4 m.p.h. On this basis the whole journey may have been of a hundred miles or more. We cannot regard this as a very certain indicator, but it is the best we can do.

After the third night the cart was drawn up at 'a large town' where the innkeeper found it impossible to understand Hugh.

This town may have been Dundalk. At the rate of 2 m.p.h. it would have taken the travellers about ten hours to travel from there to Drogheda. Unless the story of Hugh's journey is pure invention, we may propose Dundalk as a likely stopping place. Beyond this, we are once again in the realms of speculation, but we might at this point turn to the demographic evidence explored at the start of this chapter. Here we saw that the Bruntys and Pruntys, as a clan, hailed originally from the central/north west of Ulster; from the Erne valley, the district round Clones and the corridor from there to Armagh. Perhaps Hugh's father, driven out of his inheritance near the Boyne by the grasping Welsh, had retreated to the Ó Pronntaigh heartland.

From Dundalk to the north and west many roads could lead towards Hugh's early home. It is possible that the 'sea' could have been Lough Neagh, but it needs to be remembered that even a small lake can look like a sea to a small child. One of the lakes on the Erne may equally well have been Hugh's 'sea', and so could a number of smaller lakes in the uplands of County Monaghan.[24] Whether any investigation could make this clearer in future is an open question, but at least the story told by Hugh is consistent with an origin far from the east or south of Ireland, probably in an Irish-speaking area.

6 From the Boyne to Imdel

We have now examined Wright's story of the origin of Hugh Brunty, taken at the age of about eight from his early home in the central/north west part of Ulster to live on a farm in the Boyne valley. The next part of Wright's story is given as a flashback, taking us into a remoter part of the eighteenth century. To this part of the tale Wright's informants had listened with attention. We need to pay as much attention, and examine the story sceptically.

The first part of the tale concerns the discovery and adoption of Welsh (or 'Walsh', as Patrick's brother's name is spelt in his will). Working back from the likely date of Hugh's own birth, which can in turn be inferred from Patrick Brontë's remark that his marriage was 'early' though suitable (and this took place in 1776), we may place Hugh's birth at about 1755. We may guess further that 'Welsh' entered the story about 1710–1720. His discovery on board the Liverpool cattle boat is described in some detail by Wright (pp. 19–20). Cannon changes the point of arrival to Warrenpoint, but offers no evidence for this.[1] In fact, plenty of boats sailed from Drogheda to Liverpool and back, as can be seen from Liverpool Port Books and from an article 'The Anglo-Irish Livestock Trade of the Seventeenth Century', by Donald Woodward, printed in *Irish Historical Studies*, vol. 18 (1973) pp. 489–523. This shows that Drogheda was a well-known port of embarkation for cattle products, such as tallow and skins, but that at this time exports of live cattle were banned, and the ban seems to have been enforced.[2] It is possible that Cannon's alteration derives from his suspicion of the 'Boyne farm' story *in toto*, since he omits all mention of it.

It must be admitted that the foundling story and the ætiology of his name look like folk-tale. Certainly there was a ready flow of foundlings; even in 1816–25 there were ten babies found at Aghaderg, for instance. Of these, two were literally laid at the door of their presumed fathers. Though records earlier and nearer to Drogheda are hard to find, a name like Welsh could be the result of an unmarried mother making a claim on the father. It must be quite likely that any such child coming into an already existing family would be felt to be alien, and if he proved cleverer than other members of the family, dangerous.

Welsh's story also has resemblances to that of the typical foundling or changeling of legend. He comes from nowhere; he looks unlike a normal child; he makes a deal of noise; he exploits the legitimate heirs. Heathcliff is in this tradition, which has received a new lease of life in such science fiction works as John Wyndham's *The Midwich Cuckoos*. Wright stresses the darkness of Welsh and the lightness of the Bruntys: a theme to be picked up by Emily and perhaps strengthened by her knowledge of a ballad such as 'The Brown Girl'. Welsh might have been found on a cross-channel boat, but the story might well be a cover-up for an origin among the sports of an Anglo-Irish squireen. That Mrs Brunty is pictured going with her husband to Liverpool in the legend seems surprising, though it does soften the unlikeliness of a rough child being adopted into a family on which it has no claim.

Wright's account of Hugh's explanation about Welsh's name, that he looked Welsh, overlooks the fact that the literal meaning of the surname is 'of Welsh origin'. It is quite possible that in a land of patronymic surnames, a descriptive name of this kind may have been seen as retaining a positive meaning. We may think it quite likely that Welsh was in reality dark-haired and sallow, since Hugh would have remembered him very clearly, though the story of Welsh's origin was hearsay. Nevertheless, at this point the story begins to look much more like legend than truth.

It may be worth considering how and where Hugh could have heard the details of Welsh's arrival as a small child, his feud with the family, and his final usurpation of the Boyne farm. It is possible that this could have happened before he left his comfortable home, at the age of between six and eight, which we have placed in mid-west Ulster. But if this story had been stressed at this time of Hugh's young life, it seems unlikely that he would have consented to go along with his wicked uncle. It follows that Hugh picked up the tale after arriving in the Boyne valley, from local people such as Gallagher, of whom we have found traces, and from his aunt. He is represented by Wright as having formed a close friendship with his aunt, Mary Welsh, who had been one of the original Brunty children, but was probably not old enough to remember the advent of Welsh herself. It seems likely that the shape the story took in Hugh's mind would be much influenced by Mary.[3] Among other interesting points we may note that she does not seem to have tried to claim a church wedding for herself. Wright says she was married to Welsh, after her betrayal, by a 'buckle-beggar'. In her talks Mary may have exaggerated the family's former prosperity and may not even have made clear which family was prosperous, the Bruntys or Welshes/Walshes. That in the 1760s Mary, Welsh and Hugh were living in the ruins of a formerly respectable farm seems quite likely.

All this leaves the researcher into the Brontë ancestry in a world of circumstantial evidence rather than proof. Let us now look at two possible links which can provide the basis for informed guesswork. One concerns the local family called Walsh, whom I have already named; the other the poet Pádraig Ó Pronntaigh, whom Hyde asserted was Hugh's father. In the nature of things not much more than circumstantial evidence can be offered and records are hard to discover. But the coincidences are interesting, and may be significant.

Throughout the middle of the eighteenth century a squireen family named Walsh were proprietors of about 570 acres of land bordering on Monknewtown parish.[4] We hear of an Anthony Walsh, who died before 1740, and his widow Sarah, who died in 1760. By 1779 their descendant Captain Walsh was letting off the farm. This estate was situated at Ardagh, near Townley Hall. In 1727, when Henry Earl of Drogheda made his will, he left a bequest to Anthony Walsh, describing him as his 'steward': in Wright's terms, his agent. If, as I have suggested, the 'foundling on a Liverpool boat' story was a cover-up for the illegitimate child of an Irish squireen, this Anthony Walsh, or a relation, may have been the man. However, this is not all. For in Henry's will is a reference to another of his estates, not in the Boyne valley. This estate was at Ballymascanlan, near Dundalk, in which parish were situated the lime-kilns later to be called Swift McNeill's.[5]

It will soon be time to examine Ballymascanlan, the place to which Hugh runs as he leaves his cruel uncle Welsh and his aunt Mary, who has told him not only the story of his own family but also perhaps the ancient stories of King Aengus and the other heroes whose tombs, now the abode of fairies, he has been past daily. One day these hero legends will be likened by William McAlister to Classical myth. Before we turn to the north of County Louth, we need to clear up the arguments advanced concerning the location of the Boyne farm.

To put it simply: Wright may have been correctly led to believe that Hugh Brunty had once lived on a farm, ruined by 1858, in New Grange, Knowth or Dowth. Even so, there are no records of a Brunty family living on that land. But the Brunty farm, which in the eighteenth century might have been a Welsh or a Walsh farm, might have been part of the lands of the Walshes, just north of this, in Mellifont. A County Louth corn census, taken about 1740, lists 'Wo' Walsh (widow Walsh) as the proprietor of that land, far the biggest estate in this part of Tullyallen parish. She had 800 barrels of oats in her barns and storehouses.[6] This census, which is defective and in any case just misses the land on the Boyne itself, in County Meath, provides us with only one 'Prenty', at Cookstown, ten miles away.

There was a violent incident involving a certain Michael Walsh at Dowth in 1743, allegedly murdered by a member of the Netterville family, old landowners in the area. The repercussions went on in the Irish House of Lords for twenty years or more. It is possible that this murder might have been echoed in what Hugh said about the hatred of the people for their land-agent.[7] All these events and people *might* be the basis for Aunt Mary's stories told to Hugh Brunty in the long evenings when 'Welsh' was away, before Hugh left the tyranny of his uncle and Gallagher, and set out on the high road to Ballymascanlan. But it ought to be stressed that there is no proven link.

Two other points concerning the Drogheda district in the first part of the nineteenth century may be made. Both these details may well have been true *a fortiori* of the eighteenth century. Samuel Lewis, in his *Topographical Dictionary of Ireland* (1837), tells us that 'The land is in general of excellent quality . . . the pasture in the vicinity of New Grange is of the very best description.'[8] The tenancy of a farm in such a good agricultural district would be consistent with the picture painted by Wright of a Brunty family who were men of some affluence, able to live comfortably on the profits of their lush meadows.

Meanwhile Irish culture flourished. Douglas Hyde draws on the memoirs of a German traveller, J. C. Kohl, who travelled through Ireland in 1843, and was able to experience the Irish cultural life of Drogheda, 'the last genuine Irish town', where there were to be found many fluent Irish speakers.[9] An Irish priest entertained Kohl, introducing him to harpers and experts in the recital of the Irish poetry. Some of this appears to have been hero-legends in verse (Hyde identifies one of the stories as that of Aoife, Princess of the Land of Shadows), recited by a speaker whose voice was animated and moving 'when carried away by the interest of his story'. Precisely this was said by Wright about Hugh Brunty's enthusiastic delivery.

Kohl was told by the priest that 'Ossianic poetry was very abundant in the neighbourhood of Drogheda'. We have already seen that even on the conservative and matter-of-fact evidence of Alice Brontë, Hugh had grown up here, while we have found indications that Wright's more exact placing of Hugh's home, near New Grange, has some evidence to support it. When we consider that Kohl was writing in 1843, we may find it hard to discount the likelihood that Hugh Brunty heard in his youth the ancient hero-legends of Ireland, and that it was these which William McAlister relayed to William Wright in Glascar in the 1840s.

It is now time to turn to Ballymascanlan and explore there the connections of Pádraig Ó Pronntaigh, an Irish poet; Hugh Brunty, father of Patrick Brontë; and the Earls of Drogheda, masters of Anthony Walsh of Mellifont. About 1771 Hugh Prunty runs away from the Boyne and arrives in this parish, the most northern in County Louth, bordering on County Armagh. Here he takes a job at some lime-kilns situated at Mount Pleasant on the edge of the townland of Faughart or Farghart (see Map 3). (Ramsden, by the way, is wrong when he thinks that by throwing the name of Farghart into the story he has produced 'another' story of Hugh's origin, different from the lime-kiln story. He does not realise that Mount Pleasant lime-kilns are actually at Faughart.)[10]

Until 1735 the Marquis of Drogheda had owned most of Ballymascanlan, including Faughart. It is true that he never lived here, but possible that the introduction of Hugh to the area may have owed something to the Earl's agent, even if he has only heard Faughart mentioned. Also living in the area during the next decade was Pádraig Ó Pronntaigh, who in 1738 wrote an

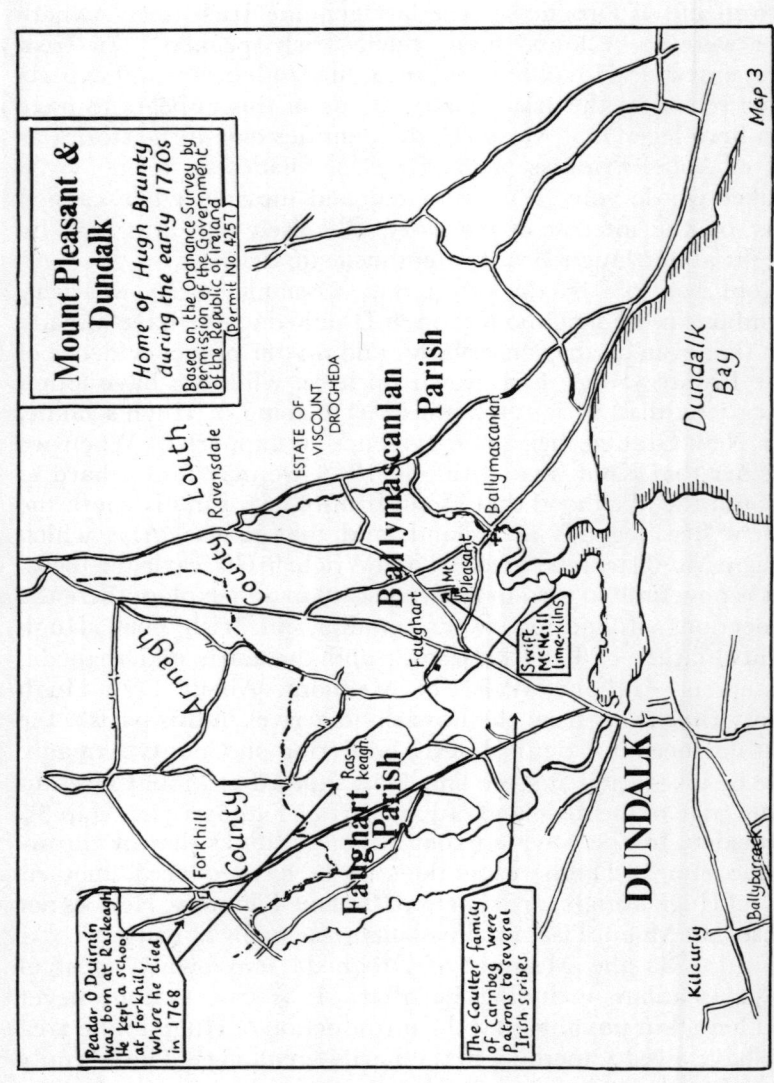

ode of welcome to the new Catholic archbishop of Armagh, Bernard McMahon. McMahon took up residence at Ballymascanlan under the pseudonym of 'Mr Ennis' to escape detection in penal times.[11] Pádraig's dates are usually given as c. 1705–63, so chronologically he could have been Hugh's father, as Douglas Hyde originally seems to suggest.[12] If Hugh was born in 1755, and Pádraig's dates are correct, and if he, in fact, was Hugh's father, then Hugh seems likely to have been the youngest child; this fits in with the general picture given in Wright of Hugh as a child with 'a large family of brothers and sisters'.[13] It is much less likely, as suggested by L. P. Murray, that Pádraig was Hugh's brother.[14] However, the coincidence of the name makes it seem on balance quite probable that Pádraig was at any rate related to Hugh. As has been shown, Prontys and Brontys were very thin on the ground in County Louth, though there is indeed a record of a John, son of Hugh Pronty, christened at Dundalk in 1743.

Dundalk and Ballymascanlan were for a long time centres of Irish literary activity. Interestingly, this strongly Celtic cultural milieu was not tied to Catholicism. In 1688 the Scots family of McNeill had played a part in the civil war and been awarded the castle at Ballymascanlan as their prize. But these Scots, as well as being Presbyterians, were Gælic speakers.[15] They were therefore far from despising Gælic culture and did not see the language as a medium to be disparaged. In 1710 the Presbyterian Synod of Ulster determined to send out nine ministers to take the Gospel to the people in Irish. Two of those chosen were from the Gælic-speaking island of Islay, the Revd Patrick Simpson and the Revd Drummond. Both are buried at Ballymascanlan. Drummond died in 1778, Simpson in 1780 at the age of ninety-nine.[16] Simpson had been given the townland of Aghaboys, in which Mount Pleasant lime-kilns are situated, and may well have been known to Hugh Brunty. Ballymascanlan and Dundalk remained a centre of Irish literary endeavour, but we need not follow the association, since we know that Hugh Brunty was in County Down by 1776.

Pádraig Ó Pronntaigh must have had a patron in Ballymascanlan. In view of his poem welcoming the Catholic archbishop, the McNeills of the castle seem unlikely to have filled this role. It is not likely that writing poems and copying out manuscripts paid his living, however, and one might see the McNeills as willing employers in a serving capacity of anyone who wrote Irish. As for Hugh, there is no doubt that a streak of Presbyterian allegiance entered his life at some point. This may possibly have been at Ballymascanlan among the associates of Drummond and Simpson, but we shall later explore the legends that suggest that his 'conversion' came at Donaghmore under the influence of the Harshaw family.

At this point in the story, Wright tells us of Hugh's efficient work at the lime-kilns and his gradual acquaintance with families from County Down, including that of 'Red' Paddy McClory, brother of Eilís. It is worth asking whether the two conversed in Irish or English. No certainty can be reached, but we can begin to guess by looking at the status of the two languages in South Down during the latter years of the eighteenth and early years of the nineteenth century. Estimates of the amount of influence Irish still had are varied. It seems quite likely that there were still Irish speakers by the time of the 1851 census, when the language question was first asked, but they answered negatively through fear. It is generally agreed, too, that the National School movement beginning in 1831 proved ruinous to the Irish language, making it seem shameful to speak it and fostering an English snobbery, traces of which are very strong in Patrick Brontë.

Perhaps the best general notion of the situation of Irish in the early nineteenth century can be gained from the letters and notes of John O'Donovan, the Irish-speaking Ordnance Survey superintendant. He combed the country for Irish speakers who could tell him accurately the Irish names of townlands which he could place on the maps being produced. His visits were carried out in 1834.[17] He described the area round Rathfriland, Castlewellan and other parts of South Down as 'the Irish district', but this did not extend far to the west or north. He found men and women who knew the old townland names in Donaghmore, Aghaderg, Annaclone and Drumballyroney, but he does not give the impression that they were always easy to find. Dean McArdle of Aghaderg (the parish in which Ballynaskeagh and Glascar are situated) thought that by then there were no Irish speakers left there. This is, however, only evidence for 1834, not for the period when Hugh Brunty arrived some sixty years earlier.

On balance, it may seem that if Hugh's father was Pádraig the poet and scribe in Irish, and if Hugh learnt some of his Gælic traditions from this source, he must have had to turn these into English so as to secure the attention of a large audience in the Brontë kiln, some of whom were of Scots extraction and some of whom had lost the native tongue. Wright does indeed say that Hugh was able to save the house from burning by the Welsh Guard by talking to the soldiers in Irish after the Battle of Ballynahinch.[18] It seems unlikely that this would move them even if they recognised its similarity to Welsh, but the tale may conceal a kernel of truth in its suggestion that Hugh spoke Irish fluently. It does by contrast suggest that the bulk of the population had already lost this by 1798.

The thesis of this book is that an Irish influence mediated via Patrick Brontë reached the four Brontë children writing in Haworth in the 1840s. In a later chapter it will be shown that the children listened to stories told by their father, and that these stories probably included the substance of some Irish folk-legends as well as tales of the rebellion of 1798. As will be seen, a plausible case can be made out for an Irish Brontë influence on the stories of the supernatural that the four children so much enjoyed. But is it possible to go further, and suggest that in addition to literary content, literary interest and style were in some way transmitted?

Cathal O'Byrne has no doubt about this. In *The Gælic Source of the Brontë Genius* he compares Irish poems and hero-legends rather uncritically with a few of Emily's poems and *Wuthering Heights*.[19] Much of his reasoning is omitted, and we cannot here evade a discussion of the nature of Irish literature in the mid-eighteenth century and ways in which the Gælic style and content could have been transmitted. Some of the detail is best dealt with in an appendix. However, the broad outlines of the argument require to be stated here, and some evidence of the nature of Irish literature as it was known and written in Dundalk and Ballymascanlan at the time when Hugh Brunty worked at the lime-kilns must be presented. We can do this by looking at the manuscripts preserved by the Presbyterians and others in Dundalk and district.

There is evidence of a strong school of poets and scribes in Louth, Meath and South Ulster in the eighteenth century.[20] The material in their manuscripts is partly traditional. For example, they copied the Táin Bó Cuailgne, a major Irish hero-legend. The setting for the legend, which is first found in a twelfth century manuscript, but probably dates from several hundred years previously, is County Louth and South Ulster. It is impossible to summarise this legendary material, which includes magic, giant heroes, warrior queens, and is full of stark emotion. However it is worth noting that it is a continuous saga, from which incidents can be chosen for telling and retelling, just as in Gondal incidents can be embroidered and retold. Although the story of the Táin Bó is in one sense in the remote past and recognised to be so, in the other sense it is timeless, just as the elements in *Wuthering Heights* are timeless. The larger-than-life characters, such as Maeve and Cuchullain, act more as forces than as individuals.[21]

There are also 'disputes', such as the 'Connspoid Úi Labhraidh agus Mhic Artáin', in which a farmer and a harper engage in an argument about the value of the harper's trade. Some of the contemporary poetry was celebratory, funeral orations, or poems of welcome and greeting; this was poetry for occasion, carefully constructed and artfully organised. Such are the works which Pádraig Ó Pronntaigh knew and transcribed. It will be seen that McAlister's memories and traditions of Hugh Brunty's tales told in the corn-kiln are of this kind. Hugh is noted for his recall of traditional legend, as well as for his interest in dispute, and the story of his own life.

Wright also has a considerable amount to say about Hugh Brunty's style of delivery. He narrated his 'romances' 'with a rugged pathos and ferocious energy which went straight to the heart, but cannot be transferred to paper'.[22] Sometimes he would speak of

> scenes so unearthly and awful that both he and his hearers were afraid to part company for the night. Frequently his neighbours could not face the darkness alone after one of Hugh's gruesome stories, and lay upon the *shelling* seeds till day dawned.[23]

Hugh's own story

> was delivered in the rhapsodic style of the ancient bards, but simple enough to be understood by the most unlettered ploughboy.[24]

His hold over his audience is clearly stated:

> He would sit long winter nights in the logie-hole of his corn-kiln, in the Emdale cottage, telling stories to an audience of rapt listeners who thronged around him.[25]

However, there was an air of mystery about him:

> Hugh Brontë was a moral teacher, and a power for good as far as his influence extended. There are still some old men living in his neighbourhood who never understood him, and who are disposed to think he was in league with the devil.[26]

This evidence shows that Hugh Brunty was an extraordinary man, a highly skilled story-teller. His art is firmly to be placed in the tradition of Irish story-tellers, and the hints given by Wright about his material suggest that this too was partly or mostly traditional. The strong impression given is of a man steeped in this Irish literary and oral tradition, as apparently was Pádraig Ó Pronntaigh. Several times Wright alleges that Hugh could not read, but this may refer only to an inability to read English. Hugh's departure from his 'comfortable home', in which he resided before the arrival of Welsh, may have been at the age of six or eight. It is quite possible that he may have learnt to read Irish before then, but whether or not he could read, it may well seem probable that part of Hugh's repertoire of legend may have been derived from his early home, wherever in Ireland this may have been.

While the proof of identification of Pádraig Ó Pronntaigh with the father of Hugh Brunty may always elude us it may be worth adding a point or two about Pádraig. In one of his manuscripts Pádraig is described as 'mhic Néill mhic Seáain etc. ón Eirne'.[27] This gives a little help with his genealogy, though not enough. But it does fit in remarkably well with Wright's late-discovered ferryman, Frank Prunty, who claimed to be a relation of the County Down Brontës, and lived at the upper end of Upper Lough Erne, near Newtownbutler. We may also recall the distribution of the name Prunty or Pronty in tithe documents and in the *Parish Valuation of Ireland*. We found that the name was most common in a corridor of land running from near Newtownbutler to Armagh. If Pádraig Ó Pronntaigh came from the Erne valley, near Newtownbutler, and Hugh was his son or another close relative, then Hugh's journey from the 'comfortable home' may have been from somewhere near Newtownbutler, and the 'sea' he describes may have been Upper Lough Erne.

Wright gives us the impression of a very rough and uneducated Hugh Brunty, meeting in the early 1770s Eilís McClory, whose home was in Ballynaskeagh near where Patrick Brontë was to be born. Hugh has no idea whether he is Catholic or Protestant. A first step on the road to religious alignment is ascribed by Wright to the Harshaws of Donaghmore, a family which was later to play a part in the early education of Patrick himself. We have seen that Wright may possibly have been wrong, in that it is possible that Hugh had already encountered Presbyterianism in Ballymascanlan. However, the tradition that Hugh had been employed by the Harshaws evidently lingered in Glascar.

Wright's account of Hugh's service at Donaghmore was neither confirmed nor denied by John Harshaw, the occupant of the family home at Ringbane during the time Wright was completing the book. 'The probability is that Hugh Brontë hired with my grandfather, whose land touched the Lough; but I fear it is too true that he passed through my grandfather's service and left no permanent record behind him', says John Harshaw.[28] In support of this, Wright says that Hugh always spoke with great gratitude of the Harshaws, and it is undeniable that Andrew Harshaw later helped Patrick. I shall be arguing later that some experience or series of experiences changed a nominal Catholic but actual pagan into an evangelical Bible-reader, and that *The Maid of Killarney* attests Patrick Brontë's knowledge of such inward conversions.

Wright claims that it was at James Harshaw's house that Hugh was taught to read, and that his reading material was the Bible. It is, of course, possible that he may have been taught to read Irish prior to this. But in addition there are chronological problems about this suggestion. James Harshaw, born 1744, is thought to be the son of Andrew Harshaw of Ballynafoy, an influential Presbyterian.[29] James Harshaw's character certainly supports the view that he might take on a servant, make him one of the family, and see that he was taught to read the Bible. According to his son, also called James, he was religious and 'truly honest'; he exhibited 'goodwill towards his fellow creatures . . .

resignation to the Divine will'. He is said to have been a humble man, for whom after his death his daughter wrote a panegyric in verse, confirming the characteristics already mentioned. Such a man might well commend a Protestant form of religion to his servants.

Unfortunately we do not know the precise dates of birth of James Harshaw Sr's children, but it is hard to see how they could have been old enough to teach Hugh Brunty to read. His eldest child was apparently William, who is said to have died 'young' in 1830. His youngest, James, previously mentioned, was born in 1799, more than twenty years after Hugh Brunty had set up his own family in the stone-built cottage at Imdel. James could have been married by about 1765, and if he had then had children older than those of whom we know, they might have reached the age of eight or nine when Hugh Brunty served their father and drove them as coachman to Donaghmore Presbyterian Meeting-house, to Warrenpoint for picnics and to other local beauty spots. It is hard to see children of this age teaching the coachman to read, though the story has some persuasive elements about it: Hugh had a good reputation with children, and might possibly have given them stories in return for tuition.

It is possible also that the Harshaws with whom Hugh served were not those of Ringbane. There are several other eligible groups of Harshaws, though none of such character so far as we know. But Andrew Harshaw of Crows Nest, Ballynafoy, who later taught Patrick Brontë, may have also taught his father to read; his character seems to have been that of a 'born teacher', though his relations with the church were not straightforward.[30] Wright tells stories, which may be entirely legendary, of messages exchanged between 'Alice' and Hugh, and locates their meetings in Loughorne rather than Ballynafoy, citing a tree long disappeared as 'Brontë's postbox', where letters were exchanged. The tree was situated near the lake to the south of Ringbane.

We may say with near certainty that Hugh Brontë became attached to some branch of the Harshaw family, and that it was from them that he learned his radical religious enthusiasm (Wright at times seems to suggest that it was somehow the other way round). It seems likely that this connection was with the good-natured James of Ringbane, but it may have been another member of the family there, or even Andrew Harshaw of Ballynafoy or his father (but this is to discount the 'Brontë postbox' tradition). At all events, at some point the Harshaws took an interest in the Brunty family. They seem to have been scholarly, radical, open-hearted and encouraging, and many were Presbyterians. It seems likely that the Bruntys received an early impetus towards evangelical Protestantism from this source, though perhaps the ground had been prepared at Ballymascanlan.

We cannot know for certain whether Wright has any backing for his story of the gradual friendship which grew between the McClory family and Hugh Brunty. According to him, Hugh married Eilís McClory after outwitting her bridegroom-to-be, Farmer Burns. His surname we shall find in the *Parish Valuation of Ireland*, his land adjoining that of the McClorys. He was a Catholic and therefore an acceptable bridegroom. Hugh, according to Wright, was not. He was neither Catholic nor Protestant, and his wandering life had left him without any idea of religion. Wright goes so far as to say that he had no knowledge of the feuding which took place between rival sects. This sounds incredible, but we need to remember that the Boyne valley is not Ulster. It is possible that Wright is correct in his implication that Hugh had no religious allegiance.

A number of witnesses agreed that Eilís McClory was very beautiful. Wright describes her 'luminous gold' hair and her pink cheeks. The courtship took some time, and letters were exchanged by depositing them in the old tree on the way to Loughorne which I have mentioned. It seems likely that the legend of family opposition to the marriage is based on a true memory. Unfortunately there is no way of testing the truth of the scene in *The Brontës in Ireland* in which the Catholic relatives try to discover whether Hugh is Catholic or Protestant.

Finally, however, Farmer Burns lost the struggle and Hugh carried Eilís away to Magherally. The marriage customs mentioned in Wright, a cavalcade of horses racing to a simulated capture; the crowds waiting to greet the winning horseman; the air of festivity in the whole village: these are confirmed by what Col. Wood-Martin tells us in his work on 'marriage by capture'. Eilís McClory was supposed to be captured by Farmer Burns that day, but in the event it seems that Hugh Brunty had already made a rendezvous with her, and by the time the racing began she was far away.

Later Brontë relatives claimed not to have heard of the runaway marriage, though it does not look as if Alice Brontë was asked about it. However, all sources acquiesce in Magherally as the wedding place. Wright's account seems to suggest without actually naming the parish church ('the Protestant Church of Magherally', pp. 104–5). Cannon, Lock and Dixon, and Haughton Crowe all assume that this Church of Ireland church was the setting, and Lock and Dixon suggest that possibly Hugh had become acquainted with William McCormick, the incumbent, during his days as curate at Rathfriland. However, McCormick was curate at Rathfriland in 1759, moving to Annaclone in 1760 and Magherally in 1766.[31] It is hard to see how Hugh could have encountered him in any of these places. But we need not lay too much stress on the religious difficulties to be encountered in being married in a Church of Ireland building, though residence by one party or the other would have been required. What does seem to be confirmed by the indications we have is that Hugh and Eilís broke a family tradition in having a Protestant marriage, and that the results of this were far-reaching.

7 Birth and Childhood of Patrick Brontë

Mrs Gaskell's account of Patrick Brontë's birth and ancestry was exceedingly sparse and relied entirely on what the old man wished to tell her. Early readers were told that Hugh Brunty 'came from the south to the north of the island, and settled in the parish of 'Ahaderg', near Loughbrickland . . . [Patrick] was born on Patrickmas day (March 17, 1777'.[1] 'Ahaderg' persists into Shorter's *Charlotte Brontë and her Circle*.[2] There is no doubt, however, that Patrick was born a few hundred yards outside the boundary of Aghaderg parish, in Imdel in the parish of Drumballyroney. It was only later that the move was made to the neighbouring parish.

It needs to be said at this point that the state of religion in Ireland greatly complicated the parochial system and in this instance makes the geographical situation a puzzle. Irish parishes were always large, but by this period they had been amalgamated as populations gave their spiritual allegiance either to Presbyterian or Catholic or substantially declined. Drumballyroney is four and a half miles as the crow flies from Imdel, and Drumgooland, with which the parish was united, is even further. On the other side of the boundary, Ballynaskeagh is contiguous with Imdel, but Aghaderg is about four miles in the other direction. Thus a very small change of residence moves an inhabitant from the care of a parish church four miles east to one four miles west. We may suppose that when asked where his family came from, Patrick Brontë replied that they lived at Ballynaskeagh, and the early biographers interpreted this to mean that he had actually been born in that parish; whereas he had, in fact, been born a few yards outside Ballynaskeagh in Imdel, in the parish of Drumballyroney.

This false trail led early writers to be sceptical about claims that Patrick had been born at 'the Brontë Kiln', but Wright's informant was clear enough. She showed him the corner of the kiln, then used as a cow byre and said, 'There is the very spot where the Rev. Patrick Brontë was born .... Numbers of great folk have asked me about his birthplace, but, och! how could I tell them that any decent man was ever born in such a place!' The earliest illustration of the kiln is a picture used as Wright's frontispiece, and reproduced by Bentley in *The Brontës and their World*.[3] This shows the original extent of the two-roomed house, with the stone gable near the road still standing. A slightly later photograph, appearing in Horsfall Turner's *Brontëana*, became the basis of later descriptions and appears in many modern works on the Brontës. Horsfall Turner agrees that the ruined cottage is 'now called the Kiln' and admits to a fastidious repulsion on inspecting it.[4] Wright, describing the house about ten years previously says,

> The house consisted of two rooms. That over which the roof still stands was without chimney, and was used as bedroom and parlour; and the outer room, from which the roof has fallen, was used as a corn-kiln and also as kitchen and reception room.[5]

There is no record of Patrick Brontë's baptism, and perhaps there never was such a record. When about to be ordained in 1805, he evidently required proof of his age and contact was made with Thomas Tighe, who had been minister of Drumballyroney since 1778. He claimed that he had been the first to start registers in the parish after a lapse of time, and that there were no registers prior to 1778.[6] The next six Brontë children were all baptised at Drumballyroney; an illustration of the register entry for William is to be found in Cannon, *The Road to Haworth* (p. 83). This is not compelling evidence of the family's religious position; there are many examples of Catholics being buried in Church of Ireland graveyards and this might extend to baptism too, especially with a minister so enthusiastic as Thomas Tighe. It does suggest, however, that there was little connection between the family and the Catholic priest.

It is not clear how long Hugh Brunty and his growing family continued to live in the small cabin opposite a track leading to Imdel fort. I have already mentioned the names of the children who succeeded Patrick into the world, and later in this chapter shall be adding detail to the outline. What is not clear is precisely where these children were born. Wright considers that several were born at Imdel, while Lock and Dixon think the family moved in 1778. A second Brontë residence, according to Wright, was on the North side of Ballynaskeagh, perhaps in Lisnacreevy townland. Whether the children were born in the kiln cottage or at Lisnacreevy, they were still in the same parish, and so baptised at Drumballyroney.

It seems to have been about 1792 between the birth of Mary and that of the twins, Sarah and Rose, that a new house was built on the Ballynaskeagh side of the boundary, near the cottage where the McClorys had lived. The land must have been rented from the McClorys. This is the house shown by Wright on page 121, described as a 'two story' house, and facing the glen across the road. Lock and Dixon say the house had five rooms, of which three were bedrooms. Although not so lofty as Haworth parsonage, it bears a resemblance to it, appearing to be a rustic version of it. It has the central door and sash windows, though the proportions are not as elegant. When Ramsden saw it in 1897 it was called 'the better house', and both then and in 1933 when Cathal O'Byrne wrote, it was inhabited by McClorys.[7] Alice was the only one of the children to be born here.

It was in this house that Patrick spent his life as a teenage student and from here that he set out to teach at Glascar and subsequently at Drumballyroney.

The building of the house suggests that by 1792 the family were prospering, though of course we do not know with whose money it was built. The impression given in Wright, and perhaps confirmed by the names of the residents in 1897 and 1933, is that the Bruntys at first succeeded through their McClory connections, and that these recalcitrant Protestants lived under the patronage of a Catholic family. Despite this advance in wealth, the Bruntys were frugal, as indeed must have been necessary to a family with ten children. Traces of this frugality are very apparent at Haworth, where Patrick Brontë never learnt to live in the style of a clergyman.

At her death Alice was said to have been 'reared on oatmeal porridge and oat griddle cakes, for which she retained a partiality to the last'. Mrs Gaskell noticed that the children at Haworth were not allowed meat, but Nancy Garrs, the Brontë servant, denied this. Certainly meat figures in Emily's 1834 diary paper.

Birth and Childhood of Patrick Brontë 67

Nevertheless the impression of Spartan conditions persists, and as for clothing, the Brontë sisters never showed great interest in fashion, while Charlotte's letters to Ellen Nussey frequently discuss mending and altering clothes. Ellen recalls that they frequently wore wool, and she suggests a connection between this and Mr Brontë's fear of fire. She noted too that their breakfast was always of oatmeal porridge, though she ascribed this to North Country habit.[8]

Wright gives a great deal of detail about the food eaten by the Brontës in Ballynaskeagh, presumably obtained from Alice or generalised from other families in the district.[9] However, so long as Hugh Brunty continued his trade of corn-roasting, at any rate before the move from Imdel, fire would be a pervasive element in the house, and the roasting would presumably extend to potatoes. A principal item of diet would also be the corn itself, turned according to Wright into a meal and stored in a barrel at one corner of the room.

The folk-artistic background to life at Imdel and Lisnacreevy, and at the house in Ballynaskeagh, would be most valuable to know about, but unfortunately can only be deduced from what appears later. The earliest evidence on the musical talents and interests of the younger generation comes in the account of an open-air dance, observed allegedly in 1812, about which we shall hear. But it must have been during their youth that Hugh and James learnt the fiddle. We have no tradition that the elder Hugh could play, though this might be consistent with his other traditional folk accomplishments. The songs and ballads sung by the Brontës sounded to the later observers like the works of Burns, who did not, however, become well known until 1786 on the publication of his early poems in the Kilmarnock Edition. It is most likely that the songs sung at Imdel were traditional forerunners of Burns' lyrics.

Hugh Brunty's narrative repertoire, which included the story of his own life, is not fully explored by Wright. He says early in the book that McAlister gave him various stories of Hugh Brunty to rewrite, but gives no clue at this point to their subject. However, in Chapter XV he considers both the content of the stories and the manner of their delivery.

It seems that when Hugh Brunty held his audience with his 'bardic' delivery, he could be speaking on one of three topics. One was the story of his own life and ancestry, as mediated perhaps through his Aunt Mary and inhabitants of the Boyne valley such as Gallagher; enough has been said about this for the moment. The second was a political and religious theory. Wright sets out Hugh's propositions in Chapter XVI of *The Brontës in Ireland*. We have no way at all of knowing whether they are authentic, but they need brief consideration.

In the first proposition, 'The Church is not Christ's', Hugh denounced the clergy, both Catholic and Protestant. He apparently mentioned an experience when he had approached a Church of Ireland clergyman but had been driven away like 'a rat'. At the time Hugh had been 'hungry, naked and bleeding'; we may assume it was during his flight through Louth towards Mount Pleasant. 'The World is not God's', Hugh added. In this he seems to have been attacking the general theory of kingship by divine right. The third proposition was 'Ireland is not the King's'. Under this heading Hugh attacked the system of landlords as evidenced in the Boyne valley, and he went further in the following proposition, that 'Irish Law is not Justice'. It could thus be said, in conclusion that 'Obedience to Law is not a Duty', and 'Patriotism is not a Virtue'. If these propositions adequately represent Hugh Brunty's belief, it is not surprising that William is found fighting at Ballynahinch, and we may think it likely that Patrick too was well aware of these views. In the end he repudiated them, but both the views themselves and their logical expression may have had an effect on the younger generation at Haworth. The revolutionary character of the opposition to Gondal's monarchs may also have some roots in this theory.

The third theme on which Hugh Brunty held forth was the area of legend. Wright gives us only small clues as to the content of these legendary stories. They were sometimes 'rough in texture'.[10] They could be 'interspersed with emphatic expletives'. (In the letter to Rose Heslip, already mentioned, Wright says that one of the Brontës had been heard to swear by 'the hind leg of the holy ghost'.) But they

> always had a healthy, moral bearing. As a genuine Irishman, he never used an immodest word, or by gesture, phrase or innuendo, suggested an impure thought. On this point all my informants were unanimous

says Wright in the passage in question.

He continues by sketching a few themes, and gives us a small clue to the type of stories these were: 'Tyranny and cruelty of every kind he denounced fiercely.' We may assume that some of the stories were martial, perhaps hero-legends. 'Faithlessness and deceit always met condign punishment in his romances'; we catch here an echo of some of the ballads of faithless lovers, including perhaps the specimens to be mentioned in the chapter on *Wuthering Heights*. 'When girls had been betrayed, either the ghost of the injured woman or the devil himself in some form wreaked unutterable vengeance on the betrayer.' The devil as avenger occurs in Irish folk-tale on a fairly wide scale, and his appearance in such a story might be one of the facets of the stories told at the Haworth breakfast table which scandalised Ellen Nussey.

When we begin to examine the educational and religious background of Patrick Brontë's childhood, we note that modern biographers are more likely to accept the truth of the tradition, though of course this is, in fact, still based almost entirely on Wright. Some additional evidence has been produced, but in essence the details of Patrick's upbringing rests on the memories of David McKee, W. J. McCracken and his mother Elizabeth Wilson, William McAlister, recalling what his father had told him, and the sundry old men whom McKay and Ramsden dismiss as ineffectual. Ramsden does indeed produce his own ancient inhabitant, Henry McFaddon of Glascar, who corroborates a number of subsidiary incidents in the lives of the Brontë uncles.[11] It is noteworthy that descendants of the Brontë uncles themselves have little to add about Patrick, and it must also be borne in mind that Alice was eighteen years younger than her clergyman brother, and in no position to remember his youth, though she may have been an inheritor of the educational and religious progress he had made and passed on to the family.

If we accept the traditional accounts of Hugh Brunty's own religious and educational stances, we may have discovered the source of Patrick's motivation both in the character and interests of his father. It seems fruitless to deny that Hugh was a person of unusually sharp intelligence and curiosity. At the lowest level we can say that he was evidently a master of oral narrative and persuasion, and that the effective pulpit oratory of Patrick Brontë, like his breakfast-time ghost stories, stemmed from the early and frequent contact with a master of the spoken word. In addition, the many testimonies to the oddness of the Brontë clan in Ireland show that they stood apart and suggest that the kernel of this apartness lay in their powerful enthusiasm, their unconventional approach, their lack of clear religious or political affiliation and their superior artistic sense. Patrick was a product of this unusual family, but he also accentuated its oddness.

It is surely very extraordinary that in a district where religious dogma and partisanship is notorious for its divisive hold on the population, almost every sect claims the Brontës. Patrick Brontë's own religious position might be thought clear: he was an Evangelical member of the Church of England and Ireland. Yet so often he retreats from the opportunities for bigotry which such a position provides. Examples of his toleration of Nonconformity are well documented, though he insisted staunchly on such institutions as church rates. Charlotte may well be less tolerant than her father when she attacks Nonconformists in *Shirley*. On the other hand, some strange impulse took her to confession in a Catholic church in Brussels. Of the four Brontë children, she may have been the most orthodox; but Anne thought her way to Universalism, Branwell was a staunch agnostic despite his teaching in Sunday school, and Emily's religion was more that of Shelley than Wilberforce or Wesley. Even Maria, who died aged eleven or twelve, has left on record the strong impression of personal and possibly unorthodox religious conviction. We cannot say that Wright imports his information of the Brontës' religious unorthodoxy from other writers on the family, for this is not stressed in nineteenth-century writers, and indeed every effort of Alice Brontë and Brontë descendants in Ireland seems to have been exerted to soften the shameful impression.

The position may be summarised thus. Wright and the anonymous writer in *The Banbridge Chronicle* (quoting J. B. Lusk) report traditions that the Brontës in Ireland were Catholics.[12] Wright also stresses Presbyterian connections such as those with Andrew Harshaw, Samuel Barber, and the Glascar Meeting. Elsie Harrison considers that Methodism was 'the clue to the Brontës', and we know that the Brontës were christened in the Church of Ireland, and that Patrick Brontë ministered at Church of England churches after ordination into the established church. We may conveniently take the evidence for Brunty and Brontë affiliations to these various bodies in the order just adopted.

No one ever suggests that the McClory family were other than Catholic during the time of Patrick Brontë, though Horsfall Turner maintains that there were more Protestant than Catholic McClorys in the 1890s.¹³ Wright's view of the wedding of Hugh Brunty to Eilís McClory is that it was a 'mixed' marriage in a Church of Ireland church. However, there is no real evidence that the Brunty family too were not nominally Catholic. There is no strong evidence to suggest that they were, but in general the notion that they were Protestant seems to be reading back Patrick Brontë's religion to the eighteenth century. The Church of Ireland wedding and subsequent baptisms may not mean much, for there are many cases of such ceremonies taking place, and the Evangelical role of Thomas Tighe has already been noted.

On the positive side, the article from *The Banbridge Chronicle* records J. B. Lusk as saying: 'I had people tell me they were all Roman Catholics and only became Prostestants when Patrick was ordained in the English church.' In the forays which took place on 12 July, 'the Brontës, with their mother, old "Ayles" . . . seem to have taken the Roman Catholic (thresher) side'.¹⁴ Wright, too, records an informant of J. B. Lusk, Mr Frazer, then 'over ninety-two years of age' to the effect that

> the Brontës were for a time Catholics. He gives the following account of Patrick's conversion: 'He was weaving in the house of Robert Donald, a Presbyterian, and a very pious man. Donald conducted family worship every morning and night. Patrick overheard him reading and praying. He became interested, asked questions, and finally ended by becoming a Protestant.'¹⁵

As we shall see, in *The Maid of Killarney* Patrick Brontë shows what may be first-hand knowledge of a Catholic funeral, and one of his characters is a Catholic touched by Evangelicalism but who nevertheless wishes to die a Catholic. Throughout his version of Hugh Brunty's story, Wright alludes to his alienation from conventional religion, ascribing this to the night when Hugh was wrested from the bosom of his real parents by an unkind uncle. This may at least reflect a rootlessness which would be accounted for by Hugh's travelling, and we also have the suggestion that the elder Harshaws of Ringbane first interested an illiterate but highly intelligent youth in Christianity. Prior to that Hugh may well have been a lapsed Catholic.

From Catholic to Presbyterian may seem a considerable step. We may recall that in the eighteenth century both opposed the Church of Ireland, whose clergy Wright portrays in Chapter XXV as having 'little sympathy with the people'.[16] One may also see social progress in the conversion first from Catholicism to Presbyterianism, then to the Anglican fold, though doubtless this is to over-simplify and may well be denied. Ramsden objects strongly to the Presbyterian emphasis in *The Brontës in Ireland*, but it cannot be doubted that Presbyterianism had a hold on Patrick Brontë for a time. The Brontë uncles turned to David McKee in the 1850s because he was a local figure of eminence, but the link between Patrick and Glascar is quite certain and much antedates any of Wright's investigations.

Presbyterianism dominated eighteenth-century Protestantism in Northern Ireland, and was no less strong in the area between Rathfriland and Banbridge than elsewhere. In part this was due to the persistance in religion of the descendants of Scottish immigrants, but until the arrival of Wesley on the scene, there was little life in the Church of Ireland, whose support, even in Ulster, was based on the allegiance of the Ascendancy and the descendants of English immigrants. Presbyterian ministers were often well-trained people of intelligence and perception, closer to their congregations than their Church of Ireland counterparts, and scholarly in their approach to matters of Scripture. There is some probability that their numbers had grown since the seventeenth century.

The census of 1659 gives a racial breakdown of property owners, showing that in the Barony of Upper Iveagh (in which the area round Rathfriland falls) the native Irish were much in the ascendant, but that there were pockets of Scots/English in Rathfriland itself and Loughbrickland. The figures are 'Ballisciagh': 0 Scots/English and 20 Irish; Glasskermore: 0 Scots/English and 18 Irish; Loughbrickland: 23 Scots/English and 17 Irish; Rathfriland: 18 Scots/English and 35 Irish; and 'Ballynefoy': 5 Scots/English and 22 Irish.[17] By 1834, when the first Ordnance Survey was taken, there were Catholic 'chapels' in the centres of population, Rathfriland and Loughbrickland, but in the rural townlands, isolated chapels were likely to be Presbyterian. Patrick Brontë's association with Glascar is likely to have been a matter of the proximity of the chapel, rather than a conscious choice.

Elsie Harrison, in *The Clue to the Brontës*, enthusiastically advances the claim of Wesley as a formative influence on Patrick Brontë and the Brontës deeply held Evangelicalism. Undoubtedly the Haworth Brontës thought highly of Wesley, and Anne, for example, loved Wesley's hymns. A very strong flavour of Wesley's thought can be discerned in much of Anne's writing, and in some of Charlotte's. But it must be remembered that Wesley was the harbinger of a school of Evangelicals, many of whom did not join Methodism when it emerged as a separate communion. Patrick Brontë's pronouncements in his sermons are clearly of the Evangelical party, but some of the Wesleyan influence is second rather than first hand. Miss Harrison rightly points out that Shirley, Huntingdon and Hastings (all names used in Brontë writing) are all names connected with the Methodist hagiology or demonology, but this does not necessarily mean that Patrick caught Methodism directly from Wesley in Ulster, as is suggested by Lock and Dixon. Wesley had been well received in the Rathfriland area, both by Presbyterian Samuel Barber and Anglican Thomas Tighe, but he did not found his own chapels in the area, indeed he had no need or wish to.

It is suggested by Miss Harrison that Welsh Brontë, Patrick's brother, may have been named after Thomas Walsh, an Irish-speaking convert of Wesley's, who had taken the gospel in Irish to the people in the south-west, and had been attacked in a riot in the Mourne district. This theory appears to have originated with Maggie Shannon.[18] If it were true it would suggest Methodist or Evangelical enthusiasm on the part of Hugh Brunty. However, this Evangelicalism may also have been mediated through Thomas Tighe.

By the late nineteenth century the Brontës' own view of themselves had undergone a considerable measure of elevation. Welsh Brontë Jr attended Annaclone or Drumballyroney churches; Alice, Patrick's sister, went to Aghaderg Parish church in Loughbrickland, and Turner says that both Patrick Brontë's parents were buried in Drumballyroney churchyard.[19] Now that Patrick Brontë was a minister in the Church of England, they did not waver from that church. But, as previously mentioned, they went to David McKee for advice, in the main because he lived near to them. Wright does suggest fitful attendance at

Glascar, but does not claim that they were regular there. As the nineteenth century wore on, the Brontës increasingly saw themselves as bourgeois citizens, for whom allegiance to the Church of Ireland was most fitting.

It seems opportune at this point, now that the young family of Hugh Brunty, seanchaí and homespun philosopher is complete, to recall systematically the names and known characters of those children, many of whom we have already met, and of whom we shall be hearing more as we proceed through the early years of the nineteenth century.

The eldest child was Patrick, destined to become a Church of England clergyman. There is no doubt that he was born on St Patrick's Day, 17 March 1777.[20] His name may have been given in honour of the national saint, but there had already been members of the clan called Patrick, as we have seen. Patrick's position in the family would make him an inevitable leader, and as he grew up he would be called upon to teach and care for the younger children. His first two years were spent in the close company of his parents, whose way of life would begin to change more radically when there were more than one child in the household.

William, the second child, was baptised at Drumballyroney on 16 March 1779. We have seen how he joined the United Irishmen and fought for them at the age of nineteen in 1798. It is perhaps significant that John Brontë, his grandson, told Wright 'the only portion [of *The Brontës in Ireland*] that I can honestly take exception to is the Shibeen business'. From this comment it may appear that John had heard from William of Hugh's story-telling and the farm on the Boyne, together with the account of the origin of Welsh. In general, his letter to Wright was approving, and he did not share with Rose Heslip and Maggie Shannon the wish to deny the story of Hugh's origin. One possible reason for this is that William Brontë, being the second eldest, had heard his father tell the story of Welsh, while the younger members of the family were not of an age to do so. It is also possible that the break in the story could be accounted for by the location of the story-telling in later days. Rose, Maggie and Alice Brontë gave no indication that they had heard of the 'Welsh' story: but they were all women. It is possible that the story might be passed on in a public house, or in the alleged shibeen kept by William (there was never any dispute that he kept some kind of public house). If this was so, the story might not reach female ears. It is certainly worthy of note that William's grandson does not deny the Welsh story, and hardly credible that he would not have done so if he had never heard it before, or if major details differed from what he had heard. William married Jane Shaw, and their eldest son, Hugh, interestingly married a lady thought to be called Ann May Wright, and just possibly provided another (undisclosed) source for William Wright to draw on. Many of William's descendants emigrated. He himself died at the age of eighty-three about two years before his clerical brother at Haworth.

The third child was Hugh, baptised on 27 May 1781. He was named after his father and perhaps earlier generations, and was to become known as 'The Giant'. He was not married. As we shall see, he visited Yorkshire and, like his brother Patrick, disported a shillelagh on his walks. On 3 November 1783 there followed James, who also did not marry. The brothers retained close family associations through their lives until Hugh died in 1863 and James in 1868. Though Horsfall Turner disputes this, there is no doubt that both were high-spirited jokers and imaginative story-tellers, 'respectable' when they chose to be, but at heart Ulster countrymen with roots deep in the folk-culture of the area.

Welsh followed, being baptised on 19 February 1786. He also lived into his eighties, dying in November 1868, aged eighty-two. He was married to Elizabeth Campbell, whose family will enter our story again, and they had two boys. More will also be said of these. Welsh was said to be 'gentlemanly though uneducated', and 'more cultured in his manner than his brothers in Ireland'. Many writers argue that if the character of Welsh the usurper had been as Hugh Brunty alleged, he would not have called a child of his own after him. These objections may misunderstand the purpose of 'naming for' older members of the family in earlier ages, where to pass on a name is not necessarily to endorse the character of the previous possessor of that name. It is most unlikely that a surname such as Welsh would be used as a christian name without a family reference. In all cases of such christenings which I can discover at Glascar or in the area in the early part of the nineteenth century, the surname used as a christian name is the surname of a close relative.

By 1786 there were five boys in the Brontë family at Lisnacreevy; five girls were to follow. Jane was baptised on 1 February 1789. According to Horsfall Turner she 'only reached the age of thirty'.[21] There is, of course, no documentary evidence of this, and we may assume he had his information from a Brontë descendant, perhaps Maggie Shannon. Jane Brontë will have died, we may say, in 1818–19. It is interesting to speculate whether Emily Jane, christened at Thornton on 20 August 1818, received her second christian name from her dead or dying aunt. There is no evidence for this, and indeed there were Janes on the Branwell side, but it is possible that the identity of name with a dead aunt may have influenced Emily's self-identification with the Irish side of her heritage. (Similarly, 'Branwell' could not easily forget his Irish ancestry, since he was known in Haworth village as Patrick.)

Mary Brontë was baptised on 1 May 1791 and lived to the age of seventy-five. She did not marry and is the recipient of one of Patrick's extant letters. The dates of birth of the other daughters are uncertain. Rose and Sarah were twins, and as we have seen Sarah married Simon Collins and lived until about 1875. Alice, born about 1796, was the youngest of the Brontë sisters. There is no record of other children dying in infancy. The family at Ballynaskeagh was a large one, able to be self-sufficient, and for this reason apparently not in close contact with neighbours. This inward-looking clannishness seems to have helped the family retain obsolete modes of thought and cling to tradition. In some ways the next generation, at Haworth, exhibits similar characteristics.

8 The Young Patrick

In his letter to Mrs Gaskell, already quoted, Patrick stated that he 'opened a public school' at the age of sixteen and continued for six years. He was sixteen in 1793. In this section we shall be considering how and where Patrick 'opened' his school and why he left it.

There is no doubt that the school to which he refers is one attached to the Presbyterian meeting-house at Glascar, a townland bordering on Ballynaskeagh and in Aghaderg parish. We have already seen two possible sources of a Presbyterian allegiance on the part of Hugh Brunty. It seems possible that the Harshaws had some influence in introducing Patrick at Glascar. It was 'the largest Seceding congregation under the synod of Ulster' according to the Ordnance Survey notes.[1] Despite its prominence, I have been unable to trace any historical pamphlet written about it, and the original records have proved elusive. My knowledge of it is largely based on a microfilm copy of an earlier transcript of the registers, the whole of which was most kindly copied out for me by Mr Alex Flanigan. The microfilmed transcript has a number of gaps, especially in the earlier portions. Spelling of names is initially erratic and superfluous information scanty.

In the late eighteenth and early nineteenth centuries between fifteen and thirty-two children a year were being baptised at Glascar. In 1831 there were thirty-four children baptised, but in the previous year there had been fifty-one. The Ordnance Survey notes state that the meeting-house could hold between four and five hundred people. It seems likely that most of the children taught by Patrick would be those of members of this congregation.

After about the turn of the century, the registers give the place of residence of the parents of children baptised. The catchment area is shown to be a wide one, stretching from Rathfriland in the south-east to Banbridge. But it does seem clear that the further-flung attendants came because other members of their family had been members of the congregation. The overwhelming majority of children baptised came from four or five townlands at the west of Drumballyroney and the same number of townlands at the east of Aghaderg and south of Annaclone. Patrick's pupils were the children of his near neighbours. Many of them had Scots surnames, such as Douglas, Baird, Robertson and Stewart; others were Irish: Quinn, Mullen, Mulligan; and a few were Northern English.

Wright attributes the setting up of the school to the Presbyterians, not to Patrick himself. He says that Patrick was a second-choice teacher, who stepped in at the last moment. He does not give the name of his informant, but we may assume that the McAlisters could have recalled what had happened at a church where they had family influence; the Presbyterian David McKee might also know. At a later stage, he became the school visitor. The Ordnance Surveyors speak of the enthusiasm of the local population for education, but the school lapsed at some point after Patrick's tenure of office.

Useful but mysterious documentary proof of Patrick's involvement in school-teaching came to light in a letter published in the *Belfast Newsletter* of 23 February 1937. Written by a local historian C. Johnston Robb, it revealed the existence of an account book belonging to John Lindsay of Bangrove. In it is an entry, 'Paid Pat Prunty, one pound, David's school bill.' This entry is dated November 1793, the year in which Patrick began work at Glascar. Bangrove is a well-appointed house near McComb's Bridge not far from Hilltown.[2] David must have been about fourteen, for in 1796 he received a commission in the Royal Downshire Militia. He served in the 18th regiment of Foot and died in the West Indies.[3] We might wonder why a member of the minor gentry should travel to be taught by Patrick among the 'children of farmers and workpeople' who according to Wright mainly made up his class.

It seems to have been at Glascar that Patrick Brontë acquired the great enthusiasm for education that informed aspects of his own life and that of his daughters. It is sometimes suggested that Charlotte, Emily and Anne took up the trade of governess purely for financial reasons or because there was nothing else for them to do. However, there is evidence that Patrick Brontë was very alive to the potential benefits of good education and that he passed on this very Irish attitude to his daughters, especially Anne. It is worth noting that he sent the two eldest girls, Maria and Elizabeth, to Mrs Mangnall's school at Wakefield. The school had a reputation for advanced educational methods, similar to those Patrick Brontë had himself evolved at Glascar. Of the other children Charlotte and Emily grew tired of education; they found actual tiresome pupils in the schoolroom too wearing. Anne on the other hand continued for five years at Thorp Green, and retained a warm relationship with her ex-pupils after leaving. One major topic of *Wildfell Hall* is education.

It seems evident that Patrick liked children. He apparently organised the schooling at Glascar in such a way that duller children could follow the kind of course best suited to them, while the able ones were stimulated to read and discuss.[4] Wright's major informant on these matters appears to have been the former Elizabeth Wilson, mother of W. J. McCracken, who had been taught by Patrick. She was able to vouch for the enthusiasm with which he pursued clever pupils, harrying their parents to allow them time from farm duties to follow knowledge. As we have already seen, Hugh Brunty also liked children, and they remembered his stories long after his death. There is a parallel in the case of Anne Brontë, one of whose pupils is recalled as having had a warm regard for her governess many years after 'Acton Bell' had died.

It ought to be made clear at this point that the school building in which Patrick taught was not the one usually featured in Brontë biographies, e.g., by Harrison in *The Clue to the Brontës* and by Cannon in *The Road to Haworth*. Such illustrations feature the National School which appears in the survey of 1854 and seems to have been built in 1844.[5] This building still remains, fronting the road near the meeting-house. Wright gives a picture of the earlier school, which was set at right angles to the road and church. His picture appears to coincide with the layout visible in the 1835 OS map, at a time when the school was in abeyance. From both map and illustration it is clear that Glascar school in the 1790s was very small, a single storey building with perhaps only one room not much bigger than a cottage parlour. It is doubtful whether much more than twenty or so pupils could be accommodated here, very much less than the number of children of the congregation, calculating by the baptismal register.

Ramsden explored the school site on his visit in 1897. He ascertained, apparently from Henry McFaddon, that the original building had been thatched and that the exact spot where it had stood was in 1897 'a blank space in the front of a house, which I understand, formerly contributed to the dimensions of the old building'.[6] This is hardly a clear comment, though as McFaddon lived in the house himself it is sure to be authoritative. It looks as though he meant that the schoolroom was attached to part of the house, and part may have been taken into the house during alterations. In any case, Patrick's school may not have been purpose-built, and we can be sure it was not large. Its discontinuance may have been due to a scandal to which we shall refer later.

The McAlisters and other Glascar trustees must have felt the need for a school at Glascar. After a break of some years, we hear of W. J. McCracken, Wright's contemporary, being educated in a school 'just opened', which had apparently started in the session rooms, and then been transferred to new buildings, presumably those mentioned above. Robert McAlister, a 'stickit' minister, was the teacher, and David McKee school visitor. The Ordnance Surveyors mention no such school in 1836. Robert McAlister's curriculum was thought of as 'pretentious'. Perhaps the ethos of the school had been based on that of Patrick's days, but without an inspired teacher.

According to Wright it was during the time that he worked as a teacher at Glascar that Patrick wrote some of the poems later published in *Cottage Poems*. In addition, he is apparently accredited with a series of 'rougher' works, which we must now glance at. A further poem is ascribed to Hugh Brunty. Three titles of the rough poems are given. They are 'The Devil in the Glen', 'The Emigrant's Lament' and Kitty's Revenge'.[7] No lines of these poems are quoted unless the half stanza at the top of page 206 and the whole stanza lower down are from 'Kitty's Revenge', as they may be. However, twelve stanzas are quoted from a long poem called 'Vision of Hell'.

The latter poem is very different in style and content from either the verses in *Cottage Poems* or the small sample from page 206. Wright introduces it by saying,

> I have hesitated as to whether I should give a characteristic specimen of Patrick Brontë's ferocious poetry, and I here

with some reluctance insert his 'Vision of Hell', written in Glascar.

There is no space to quote the whole of the poem attributed to Patrick, but it will be necessary to include two stanzas of the twelve.

> At midnight, alone, in the lonely dell,
> Through a rent I beheld the court of hell;
> I stood struck dumb by the horrid spell
> Of the tide of wailing that rose and fell . . . .
>
> At a signal they sprang from their burning bed,
> And through sulphurous fumes, by devils led,
> In mazy dances they onwards sped,
> As they followed the devils who danced ahead.

There are two factors which connect this piece, though remotely, to Irish literature. There was a long established tradition of writing about visions, apocalyptic treatments of prophecy. I have been unable to find a precise parallel to this, but Kuno Meyer published a prose vision of hell from a tenth-century manuscript which has some points of similarity. In this version, the mouth of hell is represented by a cave in a glen, as in the version alleged to be by Patrick Brontë.[8] A soul is taken into hell and allowed to see the tortures of the damned. The fiery forms of the demons are emphasised; there is storm and fire, followed by a list of crimes for which the damned are being punished. Hyde quotes a vision of hell ascribed to St Brendan, and suggests that this may in some way have influenced Dante.[9]

It is interesting that the poem begins by stating the time, 'midnight', and by calling the event seen through the rent in the glenside a 'court'. A very well-known poem in Irish, dating from 1780 or 1781, is Brian Merriman's 'The Midnight Court' in which a girl complains to Aoibhill, queen of the fairies, that she is unwed and seeks legal redress. It is possible that the superficial resemblance is a coincidence, but taken together with the fact that a 'vision' tradition had long existed in Irish literature, it may seem likely that the author of this poem had been affected at first or second hand by it, though its content is very dissimilar.

The other three poems, of which we have the bare titles and

the six lines (possibly) of one, are very different. They are apparently in the folk tradition common to poems in England, Ireland and Scotland; unlike 'The Vision of Hell' they seem to have an English background. If 'Kitty's Revenge' is the name of the poem of which Wright tells the story on pages 205–6, it seems to have been a typical country ballad of murder and ghostly revenge. 'Kitty' had been enticed to Rathfriland by a false lover on pretence of being given a wedding ring. He attempted to strangle her, but she escaped and fled. He overtook her by taking a short cut and succeeded in killing her. That night her ghost took revenge by dragging him from bed and plunging him to the bottom of the abyss. The stanza quoted by Wright runs,

> This young man he went to his bed, all in a dreadful fright,
> And Kitty's ghost appeared to him; it was an awful sight:
> She clasped her arms around him saying, 'You're a false young man,
> But now I'll be avenged of you, so do the best you can.

The story of Kitty was told, according to Wright, by Hugh Brunty in the Brontë kiln, and was well known to all the inhabitants of Glascar and Ballynaskeagh.

It is interesting that these different kinds of poem were ascribed to Patrick Brontë. In folk oral tradition, songs are frequently ascribed to individuals. It must be said at once that the ascriptions are not always valid, but they do not arise from nothing. Cecil Sharp and others give examples of singers who thought they had invented songs when they were, in fact, traditional and I have myself come across a case similar to this in the West Midlands. What cannot be doubted is that these traditional songs ascribed to specific authors at least have some connection with those authors. If they were not made up by them, they have usually been sung by them.

What seems quite likely, then, is that Hugh Brunty and his son Patrick sang or recited poems from two different traditions. One tradition was the folk tradition of poems written in English, which became widespread in the eighteenth century, the other was the Irish classic tradition. We have already seen much evidence that Hugh's stories were of this mould, and may originally have been told in Irish. Now it seems we can discern a link between Hugh, and through him Patrick, with the Irish vision tradition, as it appeared in the late eighteenth century with Brian Merriman's 'The Midnight Court'. Anne Brontë was later to produce a vision of hell in *Wildfell Hall*, in a well-known passage where Arthur accuses Helen of rejoicing in his condemnation.[10] However, there would doubtless be many other opportunities to learn of the terrors of hell and one cannot assert that Anne learnt of this from her father. It is quite likely that Patrick did not write these ballads, nor the 'vision' poem. Possibly Hugh did so. He is accredited by Wright with a ballad called 'Alice and Hugh' but the style of this seems rather late for Hugh Brunty, and in no way similar to the styles of either the folk poems or 'The Vision of Hell'.[11]

It looks as if we may suppose that Patrick Brontë was a popular teacher at Glascar, and that both he and his father were well known in local villages for ballad-singing or recital. It seems that Patrick was progressing in the knowledge of more orthodox literature too, and was acquiring books to be used in school. A clutch of these were owned by Wright. Some found their way to the Brontë Parsonage Museum, others have disappeared in the course of time.[12] These books show Patrick's increasing thirst for self-education.

The close of the Glascar school period presents us with another mystery. Wright considers it may have been in 1798, but there may be some benefit in preferring 1799 or even 1800, though this is not certain. In support of 1799 we have Patrick's letter to Mrs Gaskell, already mentioned, in which he says he was teaching for six years. The school at Dumballyroney, where he next went, was apparently built afresh in 1800, as we shall see. It seems likely that Patrick took up his post there in that year, and thus it would be in 1799–1800 that he would be unemployed. Wright's dating of this fallow year to 1797–8 contradicts both Patrick's letter and Wright's own earlier statements.[13] Elizabeth Wilson, later Mrs McCraken, is said by her son to have been six in 1798.[14] Actually, she seems to have been five, if we have not misidentified her in the register, where she seems to be baptised on 9 October 1793. Patrick is said to have pleaded that she be allowed to stay at school, but the detail of W. J. McCracken's information about his mother's place in the family may be in error.

The cause given in *The Brontës in Ireland* for Patrick's dismissal is scandalous, and Ramsden contradicts it. Wright's story is that he became over-friendly with the daughter of a local farmer of 'aristocratic tendencies', a senior pupil at the school. She reciprocated his affection, but the friendship was not approved of by the farmer. He used his influence at the church, of which he was an important member, to have Patrick dismissed.[15]

Ramsden scorns this theory.[16] 'There never were such people in the neighbourhood, with aristocratic tendencies', he remarks. However, Wright's account of the matter includes some detail about the girl in question. She had two brothers (possibly more) who were also Patrick's pupils, and had stayed on at school longer than usual, like their sister. When Patrick went away, 'Helen' had married a farmer and 'Her descendants are among the most respected people of the neighbourhood', for which reason he abstains from giving Helen's real name.[17] The girl had hair as red as Patrick's own.

It needs to be said at once that Ramsden cannot be trusted to have delved deeply enough into local lore during his brief stay in 1897 to be able to refute Wright with authority. He did visit Glascar chapel, and certainly talked to some of the congregation, but it is most unlikely that they would reveal much on such a sensitive matter. He asserts very strongly that the Revd John Rogers, newly appointed in 1798, had nothing whatever to do with the dismissal of Patrick. Nor does he advance any alternative reason for Patrick's dismissal.

It may well be that there were various factors involved in the ending of Patrick's term of office at Glascar. It will be recalled that Patrick had been a second choice as teacher, and Wright considers he had been appointed on the sole authority of Alexander Moore, the previous minister. It must be thought possible that the 'Orange' party would be on the look out for any slip on Patrick's part; quite possibly it was his energy, imagination and popularity that saved him so far. However, Alexander Moore left in 1796 to emigrate. It may be that Rogers was more inclined to a hard line against Catholics; his father, also named John, had been in the minority who had spoken and voted against the repeal of the penal laws at the 'volunteer' meeting in Dungannon in 1782. If any kind of pressure had built up among extreme Presbyterians, Rogers may perhaps have been willing to accede to it.[18]

One problem in trying to trace 'Helen' is the defective state of Glascar registers. We might set out by seeking a family or families who had more land than other members of the congregation. Such a family were the McAlisters, who appear to be owners of Derrydrummuck mill, and by 1864 own twice as much land as any other family in Glascar, as well as forty-seven acres in neighbouring Derrydrummuck.[19] In the *Parish Valuation of Ireland* we find Joseph McAlister's representatives holding the land adjacent to the chapel, including the caretaker's house. This suggests that they were patrons of the meeting-house: the 'influential' family Wright mentions. It must also be said that there is a tradition even today that the name of the mature pupil was either Fletcher or McAlister.[20]

Wright's own classical teacher was, of course, one of the McAlister family, and may well have had special knowledge of this matter. Wright checked with the McAlisters, at an unknown date, details of Hugh Brunty's story. It seems most likely that he had a very good opportunity of discovering all that it was possible to know about the reasons for the end of Patrick's teaching at Glascar. However, 'Helen' was certainly not McAlister's sister. To be of an age to be attached to Patrick in summer 1799 (Wright sets the story in the summer time), the girl would need to be born in the early years of the 1780s. She ought to be in Glascar baptism register, but it is very faulty. However, there are three sons of Robert and Jean McAlister baptised between 1781 and 1784, who may have had a young sister whose baptism (among many) is missing.

Writing to Rose Heslip in 1893, Wright speaks of talking in Ireland to a 'Mr Fletcher' as well as the Revd Lusk.[21] He may be referring to a Mr M. Fletcher who kept a 'scutch mill' at Glascar in 1887, perhaps a descendant of the Fletchers who figure in *The Parish Valuation* for 1864. It is possible that this gentleman could have passed on the tradition to him, though this must be a matter for speculation.

Glascar school now apparently lapsed. It seems possible that Patrick had developed an educational system which depended on his own personality for its implementation. When it appears again in the history of Ballynaskeagh and district, under a teacher named Robert McAlister, it will not be so well thought of. A youthful indiscretion may perhaps have been made an excuse for ridding the school of a 'Papish' teacher. It is interesting to note the hatred of Charlotte and her sisters for what they identify as 'Calvinism', including its strand of predestination. No adequate cause of this hatred has yet been propounded. Possibly Patrick's removal from Glascar by a minister who may have been more rigorous in his division of mankind into sheep and goats than his predecessor may have something to do with it.

The Irish Brontës are credited by Wright and by younger members of the family with creating and participating in a group of folk-art activities.[22] The most amply evidenced of these are the singing and possibly composition of folk-song, the playing of the fiddle, and taking part in Irish folk-dance. Much of the record of this activity is given in chapter XVIII of *The Brontës in Ireland*, which was based on a section of Wright's articles for *McClure's Magazine* in 1893.

In its original location, as in the later version, Wright surrounds the account with inverted commas. He explains in *McClure's Magazine* that the story was originally written out 'as an exercise in composition'. It purports to be a transcript taken down from the lips of the young cousin of William McAlister. It looks as if it must date from the years after 1851 when Wright was being taught by McAlister, then minister at Ryans. Its reproduction suggests that Wright may have been able to call on material from old school notebooks when writing *The Brontës in Ireland*, but that the material may have been subject to imaginative treatment. Curious changes were made by Wright during 1893, between the time when the first version appeared in *McClure's Magazine* and the appearance of *The Brontës in Ireland*. Despite these discrepancies, as we shall see, there are reasons for believing that in general Wright is giving a true picture. But the discrepancies are interesting.

The first concerns the date of the episode. In *McClure's Magazine* he dates it 1824. In *The Brontës in Ireland* this is altered to 1812. The second point is that Patrick Brontë's part in the dancing is diminished. The scene is in the Brontë glen, opposite the house in Ballynaskeagh, at harvest time. Here the Brontë aunts and uncles perform a series of Irish dances. Patrick, home on a visit from England, takes no part. But in *McClure's* Wright says,

Before he left home for England he was always one of the party, and on his visits from college and from his living he often joined in their mirth, as formerly. But on the occasion referred to by Mr McAlister, he seemed uninterested in the familiar scene.

Wright suggests that his reason was his concern for Maria and Elizabeth, who had just been sent to Cowan Bridge. However, we may consider that it is more likely that while before he entered the Church of England he may well have regarded Irish dancing as a proper activity, contact with the Evangelicals at Cambridge may have changed this view.

The problem of dating the episode is much more difficult. In chapter 9 we shall discuss a possible visit in 1812. At the moment we need to ask why Wright fixed so determinedly on 1824 in the *McClure's Magazine* article. We cannot suppose that for a composition exercise any accurate dating would be needed, and it may seem likely that McAlister and Wright placed the episode by the ages of the various participants. By 1824, William Brontë would have been forty-five and the other brothers and sisters correspondingly older than they would have been in 1812. It may be that Wright felt this would be too old for such exuberance. McAlister's cousins would also be much older than in 1812, and this may have been crucial. Wright claims to have checked the story of Hugh's journey to the Boyne with relatives of McAlister. Possibly while doing so he was alerted to the age discrepancy, and thus changed the date of the present episode. He removes from *The Brontës in Ireland* all references to Cowan Bridge and to Patrick's children. But this may have been on rereading Mrs Gaskell, who states in chapter 4 that Patrick Brontë travelled a second time to Cowan Bridge in September 1824 to take Charlotte and Emily. There are two objections to this as evidence: first, Cowan Bridge registers give 10 August as the date of Charlotte's admission; second, there is no proof that Patrick Brontë took Charlotte to school himself; the matter is still debated, Mrs E. A. Chadwick being an early writer who thinks he may not have done so.[23] We cannot rule out a visit to Imdel by Patrick Brontë in 1824, at a time when only Emily and Anne would need to remain in Haworth.

Turning to the material being sung by the Brontë family during their harvesting ceilidh, Wright quotes his Scots–Irish informant as saying that he 'caught snatches of songs which we afterwards found to be from Robert Burns'. Though Burns was a great Ulster favourite, as he was of the Haworth Brontës, it is quite likely that the listeners heard the original folk-songs from which Burns adapted his own.

Two of the incidents described in the chapter receive surprising confirmation. I shall first discuss these incidents, then mention some additional aspects of the ceilidh which gain credibility from the confirmation of these two. McAlister's cousin describes how he first saw the 'six' Brontë brothers (there can only have been four, perhaps accompanied by McClory cousins) marching across a field in step with each other until they reached a public road. When they reached the road these brothers ('all tall men') began a match of hurling a large metal ball along the road. The ball weighed about six pounds and the winner was the person who could roll it furthest along the road. 'The forms of expression were as far from commonplace as anything ever written by the gifted nieces . . . and [as] their scant education had not reduced their tongues to the conventional forms of speech, they gave utterance to their thoughts with a pent-up and concentrated energy never equalled in rugged force by the novelists.' After the match with the heavy iron ball had been concluded they returned to their harvesting.

T. G. F. Paterson, the Armagh local historian, has identified this strange game as 'long bullets', a summer and autumn game played on public roads in various parts of Ireland, but obviously unknown to the somewhat genteel McAlisters.[24] He says that in Wakefield's *Account of Ireland*, the weight of the ball is given as the same as McAlister supposed.

The second strange incident mentioned by McAlister's cousin, which can be corroborated, is the blowing of a horn as a signal to the Brontë clan. McAlister says no more than 'About six o'clock a horn was blown'.[25] Ramsden gives more detail, on the information of one of the Brontë descendants whom he met in his travels in 1897.

> In one of their many ramblings about the country, the Brontë brothers had come upon the skeleton of a buffalo, and had taken therefrom the horn. This they took home with them, and it eventually became of great service to the sisters. When the brothers were out road-making, they often used to be great distances from their dwelling, but as their horses would never eat well when away from their own stables, and the Brontës

themselves were very funny about partaking of anyone's hospitality, they always desired to return home to their meals. The sisters would therefore go up the Glen and blow the buffalo horn as a means of calling their absent brothers home.[26]

These two odd 'proceedings' as niece Charlotte might have called them, are thus well authenticated. We need to recall, as we watch Patrick Brontë's respectable career in Cambridge and the imaginative development of his family of children, that had he stayed in County Down, he might have been hurling a six-pound metal ball along the high road and producing what Ramsden describes as 'a wailing, discordant and creepy sound' on the bell end of a buffalo horn.

McAlister's description of the dance and song which follows suggests that he did not recognise the styles of traditional Irish dancing when he saw them. The brothers are described as 'whirling and spinning airily over the grass'. The girls' hair 'hung in ringlets round their shoulders, and they moved with an unconscious grace, whirling over the greensward as if they scarcely touched it'. He goes on

> There was nothing in the performance suggestive of the rough peasant or the country clown; all was exquisite grace and courtesy. The musician was also relieved from time to time, each of the brothers taking his turn at the violin.

Anyone who has seen Irish dancing will recognise the description of the small steps and speedy bobbin-like progress. It seems likely that McAlister, born into a slightly higher social group and a Scots Presbyterian background, found these Celtic dances most attractive, but also strange. Two clear characteristics emerge, which the Haworth Brontës retained: clannishness, so that no interlopers are welcomed, and a willingness to give oneself up totally to an artistic experience without considering whether it was conventional or not.

I have suggested that it was in or about 1800 that Patrick took up employment with the Revd Thomas Tighe at Drumballyroney. It is not clear how Tighe came to be his patron, or in what way he exercised his patronage. Turning back to Patrick's letter to Mrs Gaskell we find that his own account runs 'I was then a tutor in a gentleman's family.' It seems possible that Andrew Harshaw had exercised his power of recommendation again. In 1793, he had apparently recommended Patrick for the Presbyterian school at Glascar. Now that the Presbyterian link was snapped, and life in Ballynaskeagh a little difficult, he may well have suggested Patrick as teacher for an Anglican parish school, as Wright says.

But it is a matter of dispute how far he taught Tighe's own sons. In *Notes and Queries*, 5th Series, vol. 12, July 1879, a writer signing himself 'H' proposed to correct some mistakes about Patrick. This gentleman was a great-nephew of Tighe and was a close friend of one of Tighe's sons. He claimed that the position was that 'Paddy Prunty', as he was then known, 'had a school in one of his father's parishes'. 'My uncle', goes on 'H', 'saw the young man's ability, and took great pains to teach him, but he (Mr Brontë) never taught my cousins anything.' In that case, Patrick's 'tutorship' must have been a nominal one, in which he was actually taught by Thomas Tighe, but himself taught not the sons, but the children of the country people, as at Glascar. The very positive results of this process must have been one reason why Patrick continually encouraged Branwell and the girls to become educators to rich men's children. What would do well for him, however, was not suitable for the very different Branwell.

Thomas Tighe was the younger son of a very rich Irish family. He was appointed to the linked parishes of Drumgooland and Drumballyroney in 1778. Like many clergy he employed curates, and so did not live at Drumballyroney, though it seems likely that he intended to do so. In 1797 he bought land there for a glebe, a process which involved moving cottagers from their land. However, though he apparently built or renovated a house there, he himself continued to live at Parson's Hill, a little to the east of Drumballyroney.[27] ('H' says it is near Castlewellan, but by other accounts it was only a mile or so from the church.) At Parson's Hill Tighe lived simply. He had only two bedrooms and used to accommodate his overnight clerical visitors on mattresses.

At Drumballyroney the church was rebuilt in 1800 and the school too was apparently brought up to date about that time.[28] We can assume that all this effort was evidence of Tighe's determination to provide a genuine religious presence in the area. His own dedication to the modest life-style at Parson's Hill shows his serious intentions in this field, and confirms the impression of a man under the influence of enthusiasm. Elsie Harrison stresses the close connection between Tighe and Wesley.[29] There seems little doubt of the Wesleyan, or at least Evangelical, influence. Tighe was himself educated at Cambridge, and it was presumably this that made him suggest Cambridge and not Dublin for Patrick. The writer in *Notes and Queries* thinks Patrick could not have coped with the Classical curriculum, and that perhaps he was a mathematician. This does not seem to be the case, and we must assume that Tighe considered Patrick would be happier at Cambridge than in Dublin.

At this time Thomas Tighe evidently had a good library. Much of it was dissolved and carted away as junk at his death in 1821. We do not know any of the titles, but there were Latin, French and English books, some of which had been published in the seventeenth century.[30] Together with the Drumgooland vestry book, these were purchased by a Banbridge scrap dealer and kept at his shop in Scarva Street. The vestry book referred to seems to be the one containing the registration of Patrick's brothers and sisters, already mentioned. It seems likely that there was once another register, possibly including baptisms from 1763–1812, which Capt. Richard Linn found in 1874 at another Banbridge junk shop in Newry Street. However, when Patrick was about to be ordained, he sent to Tighe for a certificate of age. Tighe could find no record but states that William was baptised on 16 March 1779 and Patrick is his elder brother and 'no Register was kept of Baptisms in this Parish for time immemorial till after Sept. 1778 – when I became minister'. If this is so, it would be interesting to know what was the book Capt. Linn found at Newry Street. It is unlikely that we shall ever know; the book is said to have been cut up and used to wrap up soap in yet another Banbridge shop.[31]

9 Brontës in Ireland

In a later section we shall look at the question of visits by the Irish Brontës to Yorkshire. For the moment, we might consider the reverse matter of how often Patrick Brontë returned to County Down once he had left in 1802, and what other contacts between the families he initiated. It used to be thought that once he had left, he never returned, but all authorities now accept that he made a visit shortly after his ordination, and preached a sermon in Drumballyroney church. There are some indications that Patrick was again in Ireland in 1812, and Wright claims to have seen him on a subsequent occasion too. Letters from Patrick to the family in Ulster are extant, and one includes a mention of those which had travelled the other way.

The evidence of Patrick's preaching is contained in a letter from J. B. Lusk to Wright, on page 267 of *The Brontës in Ireland*. In it Alice Brontë is quoted as saying,

> Patrick came home after he was ordained, and preached in Ballyroney. All our friends and neighbours were there, and the church was very full. He preached a gran' sermon, and never had anything in his han' the whole time.

Mr Brontë emphasised his belief in *ex tempore* preaching in his prepared funeral sermon for William Weightman, which was an exception to his general practice. We note in Alice's comment implied respect for the inspired spoken word. Lock and Dixon consider this visit to have taken place in August/September 1806, and suppose that it was Patrick's last visit to Ireland. At the opposite pole is Wright, who claims that he returned 'not only on holiday occasions, but in times of trouble'.

We have already had cause to consider the episode reported by William McAlister's cousin, when he encountered the Brontë family holding a ceilidh in the glen during harvest-time of 1812. During his account he asserts that Patrick was present on this occasion, but did not join in the entertainment. Horsfall Turner considers this impossible, quoting Hartshead registers to show that Patrick was in Yorkshire at the time. The registers do not actually show this, and in fact may tend to support rather than deny a visit to Ireland in 1812. The evidence is complex and indecisive, but is worth summarising. In Hartshead registers, only weddings are signed by the officiating clergyman before 1813.[1] Baptisms and burials are recorded without a signature. There is a gap in the weddings between 19 July and 5 October. There is also a gap in baptisms between 12 July and 9 August. Burials are less easy to predict. There were a series of them during the period 20 July to 6 August. For these Patrick could have had a stand-in, and indeed he did apparently take some leave in April 1812, using two local clergy as locums for the weddings due to take place that month.

From 19 July to 5 October, Patrick arranged no weddings at Hartshead, and from 12 July to 9 August there were no baptisms performed at the church. Patrick could have been in Ireland between 20 July and 8 August, a period of three weeks. It is quite possible that the last part of this period might coincide with harvesting in Ballynaskeagh.

As for later visits of the kind Wright suggests, it is by no means sure that these did not take place. I have already suggested that the visit mentioned in *McClure's Magazine* may have happened in 1824. It may be argued that once Charlotte's series of letters to Ellen Nussey begin in the early 1830s, we are apprised of the doings of the whole Brontë family through them. This is certainly not the case. Charlotte was, in fact, very circumspect in the information given to her friend. If we relied on the letters alone, and the sisters' novels had never been published, we should not have learnt of them from Ellen Nussey. Ellen was not told when Anne returned from Blake Hall, nor when she set out for Thorpe Green, nor when Emily returned from Law Hill, and only told barely when Emily went there. We have to realise that though Charlotte considered Ellen a close friend, and Ellen thought she was Charlotte's closest friend, Charlotte was always concerned to keep up appearances before her, and this meant ignoring anything to do with the wild Irish connections and events which Ellen associated with spoilt breakfasts.

If Wright is correct in his claim to have seen Patrick, this may either have been in Wright's childhood, between 1842 and 1846, when Patrick had his eye operation, or also during the late 1850s, when Patrick was surely becoming too old to do much travelling. In the 1840s, Patrick was not averse to sea-travel, escorting his daughters to Belgium as he did in 1842. If he did indeed go to Ireland during one of the years of this half decade, this would not be surprising, except that one might have expected Wright to make more of the visit, at any rate if he remembered it at all clearly. Against the notion that his visits were frequent, or that they went on very long after he had settled in Yorkshire is Patrick's comment in his letter to Mary Brontë of 1 February 1859, 'Ireland must in many respects, be greatly changed from what it was when I resided in it'.

It is frequently said that Patrick sent money home on a regular basis to his mother. This may be so, but it is hard to substantiate. In his will he writes of giving 'considerable sums' to his brothers and sisters, but no letter survives in which money is enclosed for his mother. A letter to William Campbell, dated 12 November 1808, says that Patrick has heard from Ireland and that 'they are all well'.[2] The next contact by letter of which we have evidence is very much later, in 1843. Addressed to Mr Hugh Brontè at 'Ballinasceaugh Near Rathfriland' and dated 20 November, it is a letter from Patrick in which he asks for news of Ireland, where civil war is forecast.[3] He takes a strongly Protestant line, urging 'both Churchmen and dissenters' to rally against the Catholics if necessary. They need not fear their opponents because of their good cause and 'their superior intellects', the latter point reinforcing his account of the peasant woman in *The Maid of Killarney* and perhaps emphasising the distance he had himself travelled since the days of the alleged conversion by Robert Donald.

John Brontë, writing from New Zealand, quoted from two later letters written by Patrick to his relations. He dates the first 1855, though it has subsequently been dated 2 December 1858.[4] In it, Patrick writes to Hugh at Ballina, having evidently heard from Mary to the effect that Hugh was not well. He recommends that James should help on the farm and admonishes the Irish in general to 'leave off their Bible burning, murdering and quarrelling with one another', when Ireland 'instead of being a degraded country, would be one of the most respectable portions of the globe'. The second letter is to Mary and has already been quoted. Dated 1 February 1859 it notes the ill-health of 'Sara'

[Collins] and sends a postal order of £1 to provide medicine and other things. Both these letters, especially the first, with its comment that Mr Nicholls 'generally sees your letters', imply familiar if intermittent communication.[5]

In *The Brontës in Ireland*, Wright tells of various incidents in which the Brontë uncles figure. All are trivial, but they have a considerable similarity in tone to minor episodes in the Brontë novels, especially *Wuthering Heights*, and need to be taken into account in judging whether the novel may have any roots in family tradition. They may be divided into (a) tales of physical violence and (b) tales of the supernatural.

In the first category, we find a story involving Hugh Brontë at Rathfriland fair, in which details are given of a quarrel between him and a fellow yeoman. Horsfall Turner suggests this on page 291 of *Brontëana*, and it appears to have ended good humouredly, with the opponent's son, who had intended fighting Hugh, paying tribute to his rival's large stature.

Of rather more fame was the occasion when Welsh Brontë fought Sam Clarke, with the gentry laying bets on them. It may be that Branwell would be encouraged in his pugilism by such stories, and that Patrick Brontë would tell the tale with enthusiasm. We need to remember the belligerent streak in Patrick which encouraged him to carry loaded pistols, and his general love of a fight, even if only a verbal one. Horsfall Turner found confirmation of the fight when he visited Ballynaskeagh in 1897. It has originated from an instance of bullying by the Clarke family, who set upon the disabled younger brother of Elizabeth Campbell, Welsh's fiancée and later wife. (Wright calls her 'Peggy', but is correct about her surname, which we can check in the copy of Welsh's will, at Haworth.) The fighting was tough, and according to the boxing rules of the day, and it is said that when he had been soundly thrashed by Welsh, Sam Clarke became his friend for all time.

One story which Wright tells as a supernatural one is clearly another example of Hugh Brontë's macabre humour. During the potato blight, it appears that he would scoop up spades full of rotten potatoes and carry them to the edge of the Brontës' land, in the glen to the east of the main road, and present them as food for the devil. Wright makes a great deal of these episodes, describing Hugh's stance and verbal challenge to Satan. Rose Heslip played down this aspect of Hugh's sardonic humour, though she admitted to Horsfall Turner that her uncle had certainly performed such actions.[6] The story serves to underline the Brontë enthusiasm and unconventionality, as well as the boisterousness of the pranks for which Hugh in particular was well known. Such incidents should be borne in mind when evaluating the story given by Wright of Hugh's pursuit of *Jane Eyre's* reviewer.

There seems to be no doubt that the Brontë brothers, especially Hugh, liked to scare their neighbours with talk of ghosts, and that they went to considerable lengths to frighten them. Wright has a series of stories of ghosts in and around Ballynaskeagh, most of which are confirmed by other writers. These ghosts seem almost universally to have been either invented or exploited by Hugh Brontë. Maggie Shannon, for instance, confirms in *The Bookman* how the gorse bushes in Caldwell's fields were apparently set alight during the night, yet when the populace of Ballynaskeagh got up in the morning and went out to look at the fields, the gorse bushes were whole and untouched.[7] This optical illusion was performed with flint, tinder and steel, and was helped by another brother going round to the cottages to pull the legs of the cottagers as they watched.

Rose Heslip confirmed that the Brontës made use of a hollowed-out turnip, with a candle burning inside it, to terrify neighbours to whom they went at night, demanding food or money.[8] Wright tells various tales of the glen across the road from the McClory dwelling, later inhabited by the Brontës. It was haunted by a drowned lover, a headless horseman, and a man who had committed suicide. A more detailed and more disputed story concerns the mill near the Brontë kiln, occupied in Wright's time by a Mr Radcliffe, which Hugh Brontë undertook to exorcise. This he did, according to Wright, with a sword and a Bible.

Wright's treatment of this series of supernatural stories is serious, but subsequent informants such as Rose Heslip and Maggie Shannon seem to have understood the matter better in seeing the Brontës as showmen, determined to make the local ghost stories come alive. At the root of their attitude seems to have been intense aural and visual imagination, and a great capacity for wild joking. The whole attitude seems to have been one shared by their brother in Haworth, whose effect on Ellen Nussey was to frighten her to sickness. The capacity in question seems to be the ability to throw oneself wholeheartedly into an imaginary situation and believe one's own creation. This is, of course, precisely the gift of the four Brontë children, playing at 'the plays of the islanders', or Gondal. This throws light on Patrick Brontë's terrifying breakfast-time entertainment, and on Emily's ability to live her own creation in her poems. It may also be worth projecting the gift backward to Hugh Brunty, and recall that his view of himself as a child cast out by a wicked uncle, himself an outcast changeling, could be in part his own creation, believed in with an intense imagination. The whole matter also affords a sidelight on our worthy guide to the Brontës in Ireland, Dr William Wright, whose serious mind may perhaps be led along false trails by the will-o'-the-wisp of Hugh Brunty's narrative candour. However, it is worth noting that none of the Brontë brothers ever creates a myth from scratch, or performs a brand new ritual: the ghosts are traditional ghosts, brought to life by the Brontë illusionists.

Before leaving Ulster for Haworth, to see how much of their Irish heritage was known to the Brontë children in Yorkshire, it may be as well to consider two final areas of documentary evidence for the names and landholdings of the inhabitants of Imdel, Glascar and Ballynaskeagh during the nineteenth century. We have already used the Ordnance Survey and Griffith's *Parish Valuation of Ireland* to provide accurate records of the farms and fields in the Boyne valley. If we add to these the Tithe Applotment and seek entries for the McClorys, Brontës, McKees and others of whom we have heard in County Down, a few corroborative details may emerge.

The Aghaderg tithe applotment was made in 1827. It shows that if 'Red' Paddy McClory, Eilís' brother, had once occupied the land opposite the 'Brontë' glen, he had now died. There are four McClorys in Ballynaskeagh: Henry, David, Owen and Hugh. (Henry's funeral is registered at Aghaderg Catholic chapel on 12 October 1840.) Likewise four Brontës occupied land in the area: James, Hugh, Walsh and Alice, all of whom have their name transcribed as 'Bronty' by the tithe officer. As suggested by Wright, William is to be found in nearby Lisnacreevy, presumably at the residence which may or may not have qualified for the label 'shibeen', but from which he certainly sold spirits.[9]

Map 4 is a sketch-plan of the area onto which has been transcribed some information from Griffith's *Parish Valuation*, and takes

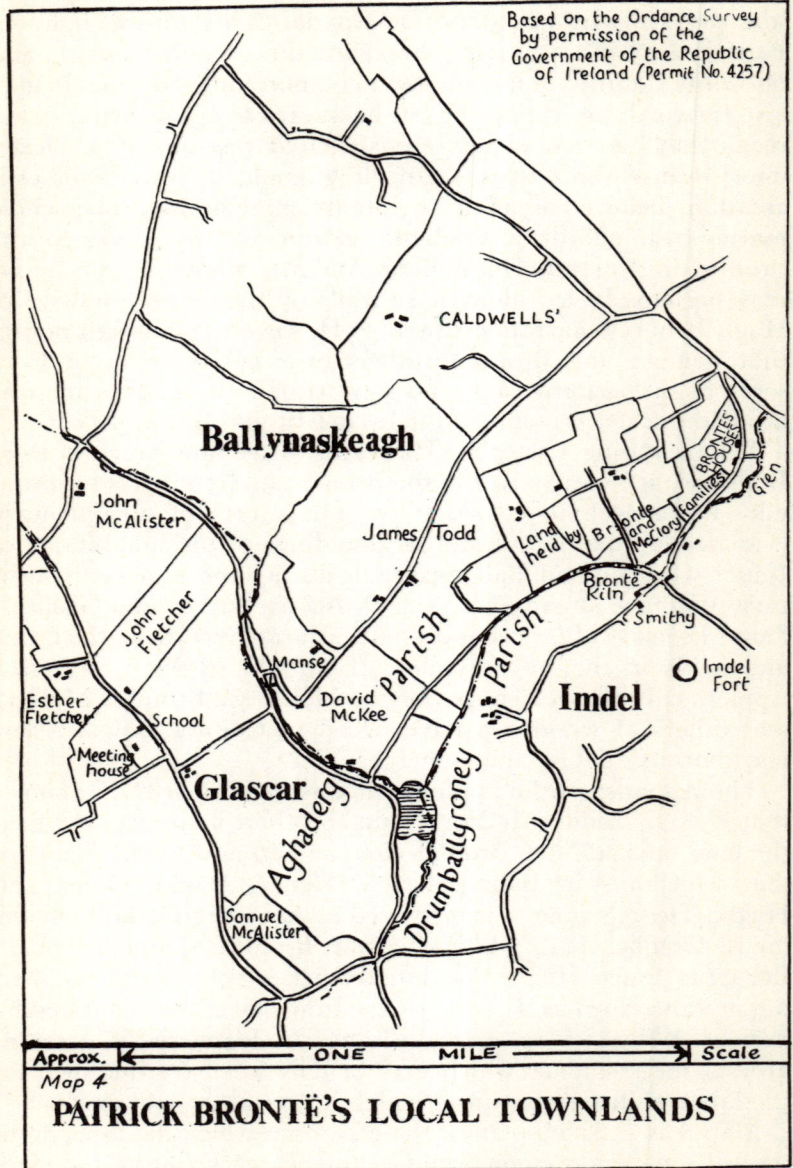

Map 4
PATRICK BRONTË'S LOCAL TOWNLANDS

into account also the information presented on page 107 of *The Brontës in Ireland*. Wright's locations of the meeting-house, Brontë kiln, smithy, McAlister's house, David McKee's manse, the Todds' house, and the dwellings of the Brontës and McClorys are confirmed by Griffith.[10] To his information we may add locations of holdings belonging to other members of the McAlister family, and the Fletchers. The land opposite the glen is held in 1864 by James and Walsh Brontë, together with William, Ellen and James McClory and Arthur Burns, doubtless a son or grandson of Joe Burns, outrun by Hugh Brunty. Other McClorys occupied land elsewhere in Ballynaskeagh.

The very high correlation between Wright's information and what we learn from Griffith should help to allay some fears about Wright's evidential accuracy.

10 Weird Irish Stories

We have seen that the Irish heritage of the Brontë children was quite different from the milieu in which they found themselves in nineteenth-century Yorkshire, unconventional and wild though the West Riding still was. In leaving Ireland for Cambridge Patrick Brontë had left one world for another. The transition was as great as to be comparable with the experience of a modern immigrant to Britain from the Punjab, who finds totally different customs and values in force at the end of his journey. Patrick Brontë had deliberately turned his face against Ireland; but it is the thesis of this book that traces of Ireland seeped through to become a significant though unrecognised factor in the lives and work of his children. In this chapter we shall examine ways in which this may have happened.

Ellen Nussey was the one external friend of the Brontë children of whom it might be said that she became intimate with the family. The Taylors were entertained at Haworth; Branwell had a wide circle of friends; Anne was visited by her ex-pupils the Robinsons: but none of these groups were accommodated as Ellen was, as part of the family for days and even weeks on end. She knew the children from their mid-teens, and though she cannot give us first-hand accounts of their childhood, she was not too late to experience the end of their upbringing, before in 1835 the family 'split up' and began to seek its fortunes in the wide world. It will be necessary to quote in full varying versions of what she told the world about Patrick Brontë's mediation of Irishness to the children.

William Wright confidently and with some exaggeration tells us,

> Miss Nussey has often told me of Patrick's power to rivet the attention of his children, and awe them with realistic description of simple scenes. All the girls used to sit in breathless silence, their prominent eyes staring out of their heads, while their father unfolded lurid scene after lurid scene; but the

greatest effect was produced on Emily, who seemed to be unconscious of everything else except her father's story, and sometimes the descriptions became so vivid, intense, and terrible, that they had to implore him to desist.[1]

It is probable that the three references in Miss A. M. F. Robinson's book to Patrick Brontë's stories also emanate from Ellen Nussey, though Miss Robinson was specifically enquiring into Emily's life and might have checked the story with Martha Brown too. Again, we shall quote the passages in full:

[Mr Bronte saw] the children seldom except at breakfast and tea, when he would amuse the elders by talking Tory politics with them, and entertain the baby, Emily, with his Irish tales of violence and horror. . . .

[In childhood] Emily cared more for fairy tales, wild, unnatural, strange fancies, suggested no doubt in some degree by her father's weird Irish stories. . . .

At breakfast next morning Ellen used to listen with shrinking amazement to the stories of wild horror that Mr Brontë loved to relate, fearful stories of superstitious Ireland, or barbarous legends of the rough dwellers on the moors; Ellen would turn pale and cold to hear them. Sometimes she marvelled as she caught sight of Emily's face, relaxed from its company rigour, while she stooped down to hand her porridge-bowl to the dog: she wore a strange expression, gratified, pleased, as though she had gained something which seemed to complete a picture in her mind.[2]

True, in her 'Reminiscences' for *Scribner's Magazine* in 1871, Ellen had not specifically connected these stories with Ireland. It must be remembered that Mrs Gaskell had painted a vivid picture of the uncouthness of Yorkshire, and it was this picture that was uppermost in the minds of the public during the 1860s. There can be no doubt that it is the same stories to which Ellen is referring in this 1871 extract, and here she makes the quite explicit connection with *Wuthering Heights* which might have given Wright justification for his link between the legend of Hugh Brunty and the novel, had he read *Scribner's*.

Mr Brontë at times would relate strange stories which had been told to him by some of the oldest inhabitants of the parish, of the lives and doings of people who had resided in far-off, out-of-the-way places, but in contiguity with Haworth, – stories which made one shiver and shrink from hearing; but they were full of grim humour and interest to Mr Brontë and his children, as revealing the characteristics of a class of the human race, and as such Emily Brontë has stereotyped them in her *Wuthering Heights*.[3]

However, the most detailed account of the breakfast-time stories is given by T. Wemyss Reid, the recipient of several letters from Ellen Nussey, who calls Patrick Brontë 'the old villain' and *Wuthering Heights* 'that dreadful book'. Reid acknowledges the 'foremost' help of Ellen, and there is no doubt that we have here one more version of her first-hand experience at the Haworth breakfast table to set against those given to A. M. F. Robinson, *Scribner's* and William Wright.

Though he habitually took his meals alone, he would often appear at the table where his daughters, with possibly their one female friend, were breakfasting, and, without joining in the repast, would entertain the little company of schoolgirls with wild legends not only relating to Yorkshire during the last century, but to that still wilder life which he had left behind him in Ireland. A cold smile would play round his mouth as he added horror to horror in his attempts to move his children; and his keen eyes sparkled with triumph when he found he had succeeded in filling them with alarm. Emily listened to these stories with bated breath, drinking them in eagerly. She could repeat them afterwards by the hour together to her sisters; and no better proof of the deep root they took in her sensitive nature can be desired, than the fact that they led her to write *Wuthering Heights*. Thus the paternal influence, strong as it was in the case of all the daughters, was particularly strong as regarded Emily; and we can gauge the nature of that influence in the weird and ghastly story which was brought forth under its shadow.[4]

We thus have six passages in which it is strongly asserted that Patrick Brontë told, with considerable power and narrative effect, weird and horrific stories to his children. The passages are not independent testimony, in that all emanate from Ellen Nussey, though A. M. F. Robinson might have been able to check the facts with Martha Brown. Ellen Nussey does not alter the basic facts of her story, and she asserts it with the confidence of an eye-witness. Let us summarise what is said.

It appears that Patrick Brontë took a story-teller's delight in regaling his children and their intimate friend with wild yarns (the 'cold smile' was perhaps part of the act). In only one of the six passages is Ireland not mentioned as the source of these stories, though there is a strong suggestion that Irish tales have been supplemented by some from Yorkshire. It is agreed that they are 'superstitious' tales of a horrific nature: we must suppose ghosts and monsters to come within these categories, but presumably unnatural actions of ordinary humans might also qualify. Ellen is sure that Emily was the most affected; she twice mentions her expression and once says that Emily listened to the stories with the expectation of finding a clue to a mystery, and that she was not disappointed.

Further, Ellen has no doubt that the stories told by Emily's father were the basis of *Wuthering Heights*. The literary judgement of a Victorian lady who calls it 'that dreadful book' need not be closely attended to, but we may assume that in reading the book Ellen found a similarity between its plot or characters or incidents, or just its general tone, and the tales she had heard at the Brontë breakfast table. Her remarks are thus in part an apologia for the sister of her friend, and are in part meant to exonerate her and to throw the blame for this shocking work onto 'the old villain'.

In evaluating this evidence for a less respectable relic in Patrick Brontë's urbane and charming character, we may recall his closeness for the first twenty years of his life to three brothers: William, who fought at and escaped from Ballynahinch, James, who dressed up as a fortune-teller and foxed the local inhabitants with pseudo-intelligence from America, and Hugh who quite certainly threw spadefuls of rotten potatoes to the devil, whether by way of joke or retaliation. Emily may have listened to these very stories from the lips of her father; however, it is possible she may have heard some of them at even closer quarters.

Ellen Nussey's first visit to Haworth was in 1833, by which

time the Brontë children were growing up. Several of the passages in A. M. F. Robinson's book emphasise that they were still children when they heard these tales, and stress Emily's absorption in them at an early age. By the time Emily was ten, in 1829, Patrick Brontë had lived in Yorkshire for seventeen years and in Haworth for ten. It is likely that his curiosity and wide travelling round his parish would lead him to encounter many tales of old Yorkshire. However, his life in Ireland had lasted for twenty-five years. Gathered during this length of time and at a very impressionable age, his store of Irish legends is likely to have been much greater than that of Yorkshire folk-lore; and this is, in fact, what Ellen Nussey and A. M. F. Robinson both appear to confirm. It really will not do to dismiss Patrick Brontë's Irish background with 'The Rev. Patrick Brontë left his Irish home early', as does Horsfall Turner.

We may think it likely that he told his family tales of various sorts. There would be 'fairy tales' of the kind so keenly recalled by Emily. These might be traditional stories watered down from Irish high culture; folk-song legends such as those which we shall later suggest Emily may have had in her mind while writing *Wuthering Heights*; alleged 'real' experiences of the Brontë uncles and their neighbours in and around Ballynaskeagh, and factual stories of the 1798 rebellion. The adventures of his next eldest brother must have been well known to Patrick and I have already noted their similarity to some of the events and scenes of Gondal.

Patrick Brontë might have suppressed the details of some of the fictional and factual Irish stories he knew, perhaps on the grounds that they were not fit for ladylike ears, or because their Irishness placed them under the same embargo that references to his Catholic ancestry did. He might have put them aside totally because they were frightening and not respectable. But according to Ellen Nussey this is exactly what he liked about them. He enjoyed frightening the children. Doubtless he also enjoyed scandalising Charlotte's rather douce and well-brought up English friend. This seems to have been precisely the same attitude as that of James and Hugh Brontë, as they tried to frighten their Ulster neighbours by pretending that there were ghosts in Caldwell's Fields.

We must next consider the visits by Patrick Brontë's brothers to Yorkshire, using information provided by Alice Brontë, Rose

Heslip, Maggie Shannon and William Wright, and mentioning the rather unhelpfully bald comment of Charlotte herself. Ellen Nussey told Horsfall Turner

> Charlotte described an uncle from Belfast, who visited them, as a staid and respectable yeoman, of good personal appearance, and she also spoke of an aunt Collins, of whom she knew little, to her regret.[5]

At the moment one need only note the apologetic tone of the comment: James Brontë – for James it was – is said to be staid and respectable, and for this Charlotte was perhaps profoundly grateful, having regard to the sort of things she had heard from her father about the Irish branch of the family. She can also take a genuine pride in his appearance, and acknowledges that he shows the same physical beauty as her father. As for James's view of her, it was rather different, as we shall see.

We can be certain that there were two visits by Irish uncles to Yorkshire after Patrick Brontë had settled down, and a further one is rumoured. The visit of James mentioned above is well authenticated, and there is no doubt that Hugh also came to England, though there are major problems about accepting Wright's extraordinary yarn about his departure from Ireland and journey to London on the trail of the *Quarterly* reviewer. It may appear that Wright's information has been muddled or conflated: some events which he first alleged took place in 1848–9 he later redated without apology to an earlier date. Nevertheless, not all his story will fit neatly into the context of the two other visits, and it will be necessary to keep an open mind about Hugh's alleged second journey.

It was Rose Heslip who best remembered Hugh Brontë's visit to England. She told *The Sketch* that he had been there when he was 'a boy'. He had been employed at corn-threshing and also in a sugar factory, and had thus earned ten guineas.[6] At Haworth he had seen Patrick and had been given ten more guineas. He had visited Robin Hood's grave while there. This story reinforced Maggie Shannon's account of the visit. She had stated that Hugh had seen the Queen in London, visited Sir John Armitage, tried on Robin Hood's helmet and been given a silver pencil case.[7] Patrick had presented one to each brother, and a silver thimble to each sister.

Ramsden adds to this story, perhaps on the authority of Maggie Shannon again, since he visited her at Ballynaskeagh in April 1897:

> Years before, when Charlotte was but a child, Hugh Brontë visited Yorkshire, and he also visited London with his brother Patrick, who took him to all the places of interest. When he returned to Ireland he took mementos from Patrick in the shape of a silver thimble for each of his sisters, and to the brothers handsome silver pencil-holders, each set in the end with a stone of different colour. It has been my good fortune to see one of these pencil-cases, which, needless to say, is greatly cherished by its owners.[8]

Ramsden continues with a story of mild Irish horror, which he does not question:

> While Hugh was in England at that time, Patrick took him to the places associated with the name of Robin Hood, and a story he told when he came back to Ireland was that of a helmet, which if placed upon the head would cause all the hair to drop off. Hugh laughingly placed the helmet upon his, and, a strange coincidence, when he got back to Ireland all his hair began to fall until there was not one left. In fact, it was as bare as an infant's. However, after a while the hair grew again.[9]

We have therefore two independent versions of Hugh's early visit to England, mediated through Wright and Ramsden but originating in Rose Heslip and Maggie Shannon. The pencil-case seen by Ramsden would be that sent to Welsh. In various respects the accounts support each other, but the date is dubious.

Rose Heslip's date may be discounted. She had lived among her aunts and uncles until her seventeenth year and had worked for Hugh; she recalled his going to England.[10] This could not have been when he was 'a boy', since Hugh Brontë was forty at the time of Rose's birth. Though we are not told in what capacity Rose worked for Hugh, she would hardly do so at all before the age of about ten, so that her memory must date from 1831–8. This accords better with Maggie Shannon's 'when Charlotte was but a child'; Charlotte was five years older than her cousin Rose and thus would be fifteen when Rose was ten.

It seems fairly clear that Hugh Brontë came to visit his brother as the culmination of a tour of harvest-work. Irish harvesters were always to be seen in the late summer and early autumn in English fields, the demand for seasonal labour being great enough to bring them across from various parts of Ireland. What sort of a stir was caused at Haworth when the labouring Hughey arrived is not clear but a legend that he was at first refused entry which Wright attaches to his supposed journey in 1848 may belong here.

Patrick took Hugh to a place well known to him, Kirklees near Hartshead, where in the grounds of the ruined priory Robin Hood was said to be buried. When Patrick had been curate at Hartshead, James Armitage had been a churchwarden and we may assume that through this connection he would have had access to the hall and its relics.[11] This would be an exciting and heady experience for the migrant harvester from County Down. It would be very useful to be able to date this visit more accurately in order to observe its influence on the three sisters and Branwell.

The journey to London is perhaps less expected, though it may be a clue to the date. If by 'the Queen' Rose Heslip meant Queen Victoria, the year must have been 1837, and indeed Charlotte is very silent about the latter half of this year. It was on 20 June 1837 that Queen Victoria was called to the throne of England, perhaps just in time to be seen in state by Hugh Brontë and his parson brother. However, we cannot be sure that Rose Heslip understood for certain which queen Hugh had seen, and it may be argued that a date in 1837 would be too late for Charlotte to be considered 'a child'.

It was about ten years later that James Brontë called to see his brother. Wright annexed some of the events of the visit to his account of Hugh's alleged late visit, but, as mentioned above, corrected this in *The Bookman* without acknowledging his former mistake explicitly. His source at this time was Alice Brontë as interviewed by J. B. Lusk:

> Jamie was over in England with Patrick and he told them about Charlotte when he came back. He said, 'She was terrible sharp and inquisitive. She was fit for nothing but ornamenting a parlour.' Charlotte asked particularly about the Knock Hill and Lough Neagh. . . . Ann, the youngest,

wanted to come home with Jamie. He thought it queer that she called Ireland home.

No mention is made of Emily here.

Rose Heslip gave another account of this visit in *The Sketch*. She reported that Jamie had considered Charlotte 'very inquisitive and wanted a heap of news'. She had a 'very wee foot and small arms and was "sighted" [dim of sight] but her eyes were as clear as diamonds'. (We may recall the 'glittering eyes' of Jane Eyre in the bedroom mirror.) Charlotte's impression of the 'staid' Jamie has already been mentioned. Wright's version of this observation of Jamie's was that Charlotte 'had eyes that looked through you'.[12] He adds Jamie's impression of Branwell, that he was 'too small and fantastic, and a chatterer, and could not drink more than two glasses of whiskey at the Black Bull without making a fool of himself'. In fact, Wright continues, 'Jamie, during a visit, had to carry Branwell home more than once from that refuge of the thirsty.'

Recalling Wright's hyperbole in the case of Ellen Nussey, who 'often' told him (though they only met once) of the frightening tales of Patrick Brontë, we can disregard that 'more than once'. Nevertheless, we can accept that Jamie was at Haworth, that he met Charlotte, Anne and Branwell there, and that he formed his impressions of the youngsters, just as Charlotte formed her impression of her respectable yeoman uncle. Wright transfers one or more episodes associated with this visit to the alleged visit of Hugh on the track of the reviewer. The most interesting is the expanded version of Anne's parting remarks:

> [She] talked of accompanying him to Ireland, which she spoke of as 'home'. At parting she threw her long slender arms round his neck, and called him her noble uncle.[13]

Wright also transfers Charlotte's questions about The Knock and Lough Neagh to Hugh's alleged final visit, but silently retracts this in his article for *The Bookman*.

We may perhaps at this stage extract one comment from Wright's book on the probable timing of Jamie's visit. He describes it as 'a short time' previous to Hugh's expedition on the track of the reviewer, which he dates to late 1848/early 1849.[14] This fits quite well with the information of Alice Brontë and Rose Heslip, on which the above account of Jamie's visit has been based. Branwell left Thorp Green in June 1845 and from then on was frequently found in a state of incapacity in The Black Bull. Anne was also permanently at home from the same month. Jamie's visit was therefore after mid-1845 and before September 1848 when Branwell died.

Narrowing the date down further involves conjecture and the danger of a circular argument. It will be recalled that Jamie had once dressed himself as a fortune-teller and played a trick on his neighbours in a manner highly reminiscent of *Jane Eyre*. We have no idea when this was, and it may have been at a time when Patrick Brontë was at home with his brothers. It must at least be a possibility, however, that the story was first told, or perhaps reminisced over, during the visit in question, and that Charlotte with her eyes that looked through you and her curiosity took it in for future use. *Jane Eyre* was begun in September 1846, after a summer when Branwell had been at his worst.

The purpose of Jamie's visit is not clear. It is worth bearing in mind, however, that 1846 was a bad year for famine in Ireland. It is true that Ulster suffered much less than other parts of the island, but potato blight was not absent, as the story of Hugh Brontë and the spadefuls of bad potato given to the devil make clear.[15] It may well be that the Ulster family would consider the time ripe for another re-awakening of a connection that had provided silver guineas in the past. The possibility that James Brontë contributed unwittingly to *Jane Eyre* is an interesting one.

We next turn to what Wright summarised as 'one of the strangest undertakings within the whole range of literary adventure', the supposed visit of Hugh Brontë to England in 1848–9, with the aim of chastising an unfriendly reviewer of *Jane Eyre*. Wright clearly had some doubts about the story, for on page 292 of *The Brontës in Ireland* he gives two of his sources. As is unfortunately the case with the final generation of Wright's sources, those whom he used during his preparation of the book in the late 1880s and early 1890s, they allow the more sensational elements of his story to melt away, leaving only the impression that it is based on something, though it is hard to tell precisely what.

The sources quoted by Wright are (i) Hugh himself, and (ii) 'A daughter of Mr McKee', i. e. Annie McKee, who subsequently became Mrs Wright. Hugh himself is most disappointing.

'I often talked with Hugh of his adventures in England, but the conversation always came to an abrupt termination if I referred to Haworth, or the object of his mission.' As usual with Wright, we may discount the 'often', and place the conversation or conversations in the years 1857–63, between the rekindling of Wright's interest in the Brontës and the death of Hugh. We may possibly infer, however, that Hugh had indeed been to Haworth, and that he had a purpose, which he considered shameful, or at any rate not to be discussed.

> Mrs Wright adds a little more. She apparently . . . tried to get this story from Hugh Brontë at first hand, but always in vain. He would talk freely enough about what he had seen in England, but grew silent and dangerous-looking when pressed as to the subject of his journey. On one occasion she said she had already heard the story from her father. He looked vexed, as if his secret had been betrayed, but he simply replied, 'Then you don't need to hear of it from me.'

This cannot be invention, but it is so vague that it leaves us wondering whether the visit referred to is the early one, possibly made in 1837, when Hugh went to England and returned with presents and lively memories, but no hair. The last humiliating circumstance, not related by Wright, may have been enough to make Hugh reluctant to talk.

It is clear that Wright's main source for the story of the avenger is David McKee, whose other main acknowledged contribution to Wright's book is the story of the arrival of a first edition copy of *Jane Eyre*. As we have seen, the likelihood is that McKee misunderstood the significance of the 1853 gift from Patrick Brontë, thinking that it was a first edition. If the Irish Brontës did not read *Jane Eyre* until 1853, Hugh could not have pursued a literary vendetta in 1848–9. We need also to remember that by the time Wright composed *The Brontës in Ireland*, McKee had died. Whatever he told Wright in the 1850s or 1860s could not be checked.

It must be admitted quite frankly that the whole story is enormously unconvincing. Angus McKay attacked it with great gusto in *The Brontës: Fact and Fiction*, a developed version of his earlier article in *The Westminster Review*. Among the more telling points he makes are that the circulation of *The Quarterly* in

Ballynaskeagh must have been small; that Hugh would have had to act very quickly to arrive at Haworth before Christmas in 1848 and have completed his mission before Charlotte discovered in February 1849 that Miss Rigby was the author of the review; that despite enquiries at the British Museum, he cannot trace any record of Hugh being admitted to the reading room, and that letters to John Murray and Smith, Elder have failed to confirm the expedition. As we have already seen, it is in any case most improbable that the Irish Brontës knew of *Jane Eyre* until 1853.

What, then, is left of a supposed mission by Hugh Brontë in 1848–9, for a secret purpose, which he refused to talk of later when asked by Wright or Mrs Wright? It is possible that Hugh only visited England once, and did not discuss this because of the unhappy result of trying on Robin Hood's helmet, or some other cause associated with the visit. On the other hand a good deal that happened on that expedition did become known, and has already been dealt with in this chapter. The evidence suggests that Hugh had been perfectly willing to talk about this journey, and despite the helmet episode, had enjoyed himself. As we have seen, a number of incidents originally annexed by Wright to this late visit of Hugh's were later transferred either to his earlier visit, or to the visit of James about 1846. Despite these grave objections, it is hard to see how we can avoid the impression that Hugh did come to England a second time.

Hugh, it appears, arrived at Haworth on a Sunday. He was at first refused entrance by a servant whom Wright calls Martha. 'The faithful old Yorkshire woman looked upon him as a tramp'. At that time Martha was twenty; it looks as if Wright means Tabitha Aykroyd. However, if the remark refers to Hugh's visit of 1837 (?), Tabby might well have answered the door, and could rightly be described as 'old'. Anne's part in the encouragement of Hugh is stressed; it must be remembered that a stronger tradition records Anne's wish to return 'home' with Jamie. Patrick Brontë is represented as condemning the expedition, as well he might, if as McKay says murder was intended. In the end Hugh left for London by himself, taking lodgings with friends of Branwell near the River Thames, and it was from here that he sallied forth to pester bookshops and publishing houses.

Wright's story is quite well constructed despite its total implausibility. The mystery is exactly what David McKee tried to tell Wright on that remote occasion thirty years previously. It may be that his story was a hoax pure and simple, intended to pull the leg of the credulous undergraduate; or it may have been based on a real visit to Haworth in the winter of 1848–9, about which Hugh Brontë was reluctant to talk. It does unfortunately strike a slightly depressing note for the biographer trying to sort out the fact and fiction in Wright's book, and emphasises how little should be taken on the evidence of Wright which cannot be verified from other sources.

Yet there is some inner consistency with what we know of the time at which the visit is supposed to have taken place, even if we discount the purpose and details of the stay in London. Charlotte and Anne are duly mentioned, Branwell and Emily omitted, for example. We might also remember that another member of the Brontë family, Branwell himself, visited London and brought back a very inaccurate account of his adventures there. It may be that it was not McKee who invented the story of the search in the publishing houses and libraries, but Hugh Brontë, a known leg-puller. In this case it may be that Branwell took after his uncle. One must remember too that Irish harvesters made annual pilgrimages to England; it is rather unusual for only one trip to be made. It may be that this second journey has been enlarged by Hugh Brontë from a real experience for a joke, which has been taken seriously by McKee and embroidered by Wright by the transference of material from other visits. In this case, the journey will have happened one summer, not during the winter, and further details will need to be modified. One small point which can be confirmed is the existence at the time of a vessel *Sea Nymph*, mentioned by Wright, by which Hugh might have travelled between Warrenpoint and Liverpool.

11 The Irish Writing of Patrick Brontë

A number of minor works attributed to Patrick Brontë have already been mentioned. There is no way of knowing whether any of these was actually composed by him, but it seems likely that he earned the reputation of being a scholar and a composer of verse, both in Anglo-Irish folk modes, and if the attribution of 'The Vision of Hell' is correct, in a style possibly derived from Irish literary sources. Throughout his long life Patrick Brontë was continuously writing and talking, telling stories and composing sermons, some of which he printed. But in the early days of his settlement in England he wrote more than he did at a later stage. We may perhaps interpret this to mean that he had thought of himself as a scholar–parson, who would contribute to theological and other topics at regional and national level. We shall now examine that part of his work where Irish influence or interests are apparent.

Cottage Poems, published in 1811, contains the best known of Patrick Brontë's verses, including 'The Irish Cabin', which may perhaps give a description of the cottage at Imdel. It is quite impossible to say when this poem was written, and we have no evidence to support the assertion by Wright that the poem was known to schoolchildren in Glascar during the 1790s.[1] The poem specifically calls the house 'the cabin of Mourne', and this is the only one of Patrick's poems in which he refers to his own region of Ireland.

> A neat Irish Cabin, snow-proof,
> Well-thatched, had a good earthen floor,
> One chimney in midst of the roof,
> One window, and one latched door.

This is an accurate description of the Brontë kiln cottage, the earliest extant picture of which shows thatch, one window, and one door (broken down by the time of the picture).

The poem tells of a traveller who arrives at the cottage in bad weather. He finds it 'compact' and 'neat', glowing with warmth, which is reflected in the warm welcome from the family. They include a 'dame', who is spinning, a father, who returns and hangs up his flail, a daughter, who leaves her 'reel' and a group of children. Furniture consists of an oaken stool, together with the spinning mechanisms already mentioned. The father greets the stranger and there is some homely religious talk. The stranger is then invited to a meal of potato and herring with 'water just fresh from the spring'. There is a section in praise of the Spartan life of cottagers, an echo of which was found at Haworth parsonage. The poem seems an accurate reflection of life in an Irish cottage, though the characters are in no sense portraits of the Brontë family in Ireland. We may note the sympathetic portrait of the young girl, a forerunner of 'Mary Bower' in *The Cottage in the Wood* (a piece otherwise apparently English) and Flora Loughlean in *The Maid of Killarney*. I have already mentioned Patrick Brontë's penchant for these romanticised portraits of young girls in reference to the alleged cause of his dismissal from Glascar. The present portrait may also owe something to the favourite sister, Jane Brontë, aged twenty-two at this time, after whose death Hugh Brontë laid aside his fiddle playing for ever.

This is certainly a romanticised portrait of life in an Irish cottage, but it does provide touches of realism. The fire, the wholesome fare, the warm-hearted welcome, would presumably be matters of fact in the Imdel cottage. As interesting is the Irish patriotism shown in this poem published in 1811. Patrick writes in the last two stanzas of forgiveness, friendship and courage as Irish virtues, but lists Irish faults as 'Dissensions, impetuous zeal / And wild prodigality'.

In 1813, Patrick Brontë produced *The Rural Minstrel*, in which the Yorkshire scene of Kirkstall Abbey is treated. Other poems include one which is very reminiscent of Gray's 'Elegy' and one ('The Distress and Relief') which looks forward to Anne's poems about sin and back (whether Patrick knew it or not) to the laments on sin of Pádraig Ó Pronntaigh. The final poem of this collection may be significant. Entitled 'The Harper of Erin', it tells of 'an ancient harper, skilled in rustic lore', who sits on a rock at Killarney and plays his harp. But he does not choose to sing 'of Erin', but instead 'I'd sing the praise of my Redeeming God'. This is the first mention in Patrick's works of Killarney, to which he will return in *The Maid of Killarney*. His choice is odd, and we may perhaps guess that for him Killarney was beginning to symbolise the acceptable and romantic aspect of Ireland while he now began to abandon the real Ireland of the north where he had been born. Erskine Stuart, researching much later for *The Brontë Country*, found that at Dewsbury he had 'talked and preached with a marked Irish accent. . . . A true son of Ulster, he wore a blue linen frock-coat reaching below the knee, and generally carried a shillelah in his hand, grasped by the middle in true Hibernian fashion. He was noted for his winning way with children.'[2] (We have seen the same winning way at Glascar, and it was also apparent in his father, Hugh.)

Nevertheless, Patrick Brontë was now married to a Cornish girl and settled in Yorkshire for good. It seems likely that in 'The Harper of Erin' he is announcing his intention to abandon Ireland as a subject. But we note the respect for the harper's previous rustic skill (as exhibited in *Cottage Poems?*). If this is a self-identification, Patrick Brontë is placing himself in the Irish literary tradition, but claiming henceforth to use this acquired skill for religious subjects. But in his one long fiction he does glance back.

Though we know of no composition date for it, Patrick Brontë's *The Maid of Killarney* was published anonymously in 1818 and only authenticated in 1860, when three clergymen visited him at Haworth and he signed a copy of the book 'thereby acknowledging the authorship of this volume'.[3] It is his longest work and is of obvious interest to those considering his Irish origins.

Perhaps the most striking episode in the book is the account of a wake. It will be necessary to consider this description in a certain amount of detail. Albion, an English visitor, has held a conversation with an old Catholic woman who has been ill for some time and has been tended by the saintly girl, Flora Loughlean. The next day he is astounded to hear that she has died. On leaving his overnight lodging he is met by an Irishman, a 'respectable looking gentleman', who asks if he is going to the wake. There is some misunderstanding here, as Albion confuses the English and Irish uses of the word. However, eventually he proceeds to the house of death with the respectable Irishman accompanying him.

They enter the small cabin where yesterday Albion met the old peasant woman. She is stretched out and covered by a white sheet, while round the corpse sit twelve old women, all but three of whom are cheerfully conversing. In the two shady corners of the cabin are some old people smoking and some young ones, men and women 'at various kinds of plays'. Shortly the old women begin keening and clapping their hands in the 'Irish Cry' which is said to be used only at the funeral of Catholics, and has Scriptural authority in the mourning of the Israelites over Jacob's remains.

Albion is astonished at the ritual and asks for an explanation and translation. He is told that the only three real mourners are those sitting at the head of the corpse; the rest are either sympathisers or hired mourners. We must quote the words of the dirge in full, since it will be possible to compare them with other examples of the genre.

> 'O! my dear honey, why did you die? Was it because they did not give you butter, and milk, and potatoes, that you left them? Was not Miss Loughlean kind to you? Open your lips, and thank her for her kindness! But you cannot look up, nor open your lips – your eyes are sealed, and your lips frozen in death! Has your dear husband met you, and welcomed you into another world? Speak, ah! speak to your dear children, whose tears are falling on your clay-cold face! Are you at last unkind? You always attended to their cries before: but now you don't hear them; and yet you seem to smile. Speak to us one word – all your friends and neighbours are around you, and yet you won't welcome them. Ah! woe – woe – is me! – If you don't mind us, send your thanks at least to Miss Flora Loughlean!' (Ch. II)

In *Traces of the Elder Faiths of Ireland* Col. W. G. Wood-Martin gives three examples of Irish lamentation.[4] One is quoted from Thomas Dineley's tour through Ireland in the seventeenth century. The tone of this is very similar to the above: the mourner upbraids the dead person for dying, asking, 'Thy friends and relations were so kind to thee, why didst thou think of dying?'

The second is quoted from George Crabbe, and appears to have a refrain, 'Cold and silent is thy bed'. This version does not address the corpse directly and on the whole seems likely to be further from the original. The third lamentation is quoted from Lady Wilde (either *Ancient Cures, Charms and Usages of Ireland* or *Ancient Legends, Mystic Charms and Superstitions of Ireland*) and is worth reproducing for comparison with Patrick Brontë's example.[5]

'O women, look on me! Look on me, women! Have you ever seen sorrow like mine? Have you ever seen the like of me in my sorrow? Arrah, then, my darling! my darling! 'tis your mother that calls you. How long you are sleeping. Do you see all the people round you, my darling, and sorely weeping? Arrah, what is this paleness on your face? Sure, there was no equal to it in Erin for beauty and fairness, and your hair was heavy as the wing of a raven, and your skin was whiter than the hand of a lady. Is it the stranger must carry me to my grave, and my son lying here?'

It will be noted that the tone of both Patrick Brontë's lament and of Lady Wilde's is of pleading and rhetoric, almost blame. Dineley's version too asks 'why is it, then, that thou are dead?' The references to the paleness of the dead person's face, the tears falling from the mourners, might be supposed likely, but it may well seem that Patrick Brontë has caught the tone of reproach found in the other versions.

It will be recalled that *The Maid of Killarney* was written in 1818, perhaps even before. At this time little folklore work had been done, as clearly appears in such bibliographies as that provided by Seán Ó Súilleabháin in *The Types of Irish Folktale* (Helsinki, 1963). As the nineteenth century proceeded, there were many small local books printed which concerned Irish customs, but even in these detailed translations of dirges were rare. Apart from Thomas Dineley's *Journal*, there does not seem to be much in print from which Patrick Brontë could have obtained his material, and it agrees well with examples collected after his day.

It must seem highly probable that as a boy Patrick Brontë had attended at wakes in County Down. Here he had heard the mourners keening, and witnessed the strange wake games briefly mentioned in his account. Such games were quite bizarre and involved drunkenness and mock weddings; Catholic priests had discouraged but could not eliminate them. One might imagine that if Patrick Brontë told funeral stories of this kind in the Haworth kitchen, Ellen Nussey might indeed feel affronted. If we accept that this passage in *The Maid of Killarney* is written from observation, it may also seem that Patrick must have known Irish, or had access to close friends who did; and he must have been close enough to a Catholic tradition to be allowed to attend. Two stories are thus given added circumstantial corroboration: that of Hugh Brunty's speaking Irish and of the family's Catholic ancestry.

The Maid of Killarney is, of course, a moral tale, the antecedent of *Agnes Grey* and *Wildfell Hall*, and the characterisation is subservient to the moral. The incidentals of the plot are of Patrick Brontë's fancy. The episode with the Whiteboys shows valour and gives an opportunity for Loughlean to treat John O'Flacharty with generous egalitarianism; Ellen Green is exhibited as an example of honest simplicity, and might owe something to Scott's Madge Wildfire if *Heart of Midlothian* had been published a little earlier; but there is no real reason why she should be given a fierce dog called Lion. Among the poor cottagers relieved by Flora is Jenny, the mother of twins; her husband is a teacher (a trade known to Patrick Brontë), but this adds nothing to the moral.

Death is important for Patrick Brontë's novel. Nanny, though a Catholic who 'would not die any other for the world' despite her Evangelical conversion, is contrasted favourably with John Saville, a member of Dr Burnet's flock, and with the miserable Betty. The admirable Flora may remind us of Maria Branwell, later Mrs Brontë, while Captain Loughlean and Dr O'Leary are Irish lay figures. The outline of the story is unoriginal, the didactic purpose paramount.

I should, however, like to focus on two episodes which are not particularly germane to the plot, the first of which I have mentioned above. This is the introduction into the story gratuitously of a fierce dog; the other is the return of Albion to England, necessary to allow a conventional testing time for the love between himself and Flora.

Ellen Green is said to be 'blameless and pious', but 'evidently not in her right mind'. She has been pursued by village children and had turf and stones thrown at her. The throwing of turf is worth noting, as adding an authentic detail perhaps recalled from Patrick's youth. She is rescued by the Loughleans, and allowed to live in a humble cottage on their estate. Her simplicity attracts a 'very fierce dog', who becomes 'her faithful and formidable guard'. 'Lion' has a red ribbon round his neck, and pulls a small cart. Telling why she keeps the dog, Ellen says, 'He is a faithful and steady friend, and loves me, I love him, and sometimes when I am hungry, I divide my bit of bread with him, and he is grateful for it, and would fight for me till he would die.' We learn that Ellen was given the dog by Loughlean and that the two have become inseparable.

The dramatic date of the novel is 1817, and it was published in 1818, the year of Emily Brontë's birth. Yet we cannot fail to note the similarity between the imaginary dog in the story and the real Keeper whom Emily befriended despite his ferocity. As so often with the Brontës, we get the sense of them somehow living their own books. We recall that in *Shirley* Charlotte allows the heroine a similar relationship with her dog as Emily had; and so Patrick Brontë's story anticipates Emily's Keeper, and Keeper anticipates Tartar. Is it possible that Ellen Green's dog is himself based on a real dog?

According to Wright, Hugh Brunty told of his own relationship to a fierce dog who 'for years never lost sight of his master' but who had to be left behind in the Boyne valley when he escaped to freedom. Like Lion and Tartar, this dog (alleged by Wright also to be called Keeper) protected his human friend through all assaults and arguments, licked him when he was ill, and remained totally faithful. Patrick had no need to give Ellen Green a dog; in fact Ellen is not vital to the plot and Lion is quite inessential. If he did so, this may have been because the story of Hugh and his dog was well known to him, or because he had adopted his enthusiasm for large and unruly dogs from his father.

The second episode in which Patrick Brontë gives details which are curious and unnecessary to his plot is that in which Albion returns to England for a while. As has already been said, it is necessary for Albion to retire off-stage, so that his love for Flora, and hers for him, shall be tested. The mechanism for this period of absence is worth looking at. Albion is at his inn one evening when a letter is brought to him 'urging his speedy return to England, to settle his accounts, and transact business of importance, connected with his father's death, which had taken place about two years before'.

We have not been introduced to Albion's father, and the information that he has died two years ago seems quite gratuitous. It may seem surprising that so long a time had elapsed between the death and the settlement, and perhaps almost equally surprising that any such detail should be included at all. I have already suggested in chapter 9 that Patrick Brontë may have returned for a visit to Ballynaskeagh in 1812, during the months of July and August. On 26 August Maria Branwell addressed a letter to him which shows that their friendship had reached a new phase. It may be that Albion's return to England before a new phase was reached in his courtship of the Irish Flora mirrors a return to Ireland by Patrick on the eve of the new stage in his own courtship.

The date of Hugh Brunty's death is conjectural, but is generally thought to be 1808. It is possible that Patrick's visit in 1812 was a final stage in clearing up his father's affairs, some years after his death. If so, then Patrick may be using his own circumstances in this episode of the book, just as he used the Catholic wake and the faithfulness of his father's dog. Unless this is so, there seems no good reason for introducing Albion's father, or mentioning his death.

Two other features of *The Maid of Killarney* are worth mentioning. They are the general tendency for dispute, leading to O'Leary's attempts to define the Irish character. A considerable proportion of the book is polemic, but not religious polemic alone. In chapter 4, Dr O'Leary makes a sustained criticism of the British legal system. In particular, he lays stress on the difficulty of understanding the laws, with their 'tautology and perplexity without end'. O'Leary objects firmly to the sentencing policy which leads a sheep-stealer, since he can be hanged for his crime, to add murder to it. The style of argument looks quite similar to that alleged by Wright of Hugh Brunty, though in his case the position of Ireland under the crown is the issue.

It is also interesting to see what Patrick Brontë considered to be the Irish character. Near the beginning of chapter 1 he allows Albion to give his view that 'the Irish are free, humorous, and designing; their courage is sometimes rash and their liberality often prodigal: many of them are interesting and original'. This is subsequently modified to apply particularly to 'the palace [rather] than . . . the cottage'. Nevertheless, it is interesting that Patrick identifies a number of characteristics as Irish which he regards himself as possessing.

It may well seem that in 1818 Patrick Brontë had by no means jettisoned his Irish feeling and nationality. The tradition that he used a shillelagh during his Hartshead ministry appears in several books. An episode recorded in Scruton's *Thornton and the Brontës* emphasises the continuity of his character from his days at Glascar school.[6] A March snowstorm interrupted a procession of sixty children whom Patrick Brontë was taking to Bradford for confirmation. Patrick is said to have rushed into the Talbot Hotel and ordered hot dinners for the whole band to be prepared for when the service was over. It was still snowing by then, but he led his flock into the inn, where they stayed and warmed themselves for three or four hours until the snow stopped. This care for the young people, the leading them in person on expeditions, seems very like the accounts Wright gives of days in the Mourne mountains, though Wright could not have read Scruton's book. By the time *Killarney* was published, Charlotte was three and Emily either just born or just about to be so. Neither Patrick's Irishness nor his entertaining concern for children had waned by this time, despite the declaration in 'The Harper of Erin'.

In a much later work, *Signs of the Times*, published in 1835, Patrick Brontë argues against the disestablishment of the Church. Throughout the argument he calls his Church 'The Church of England and Ireland'. Part of his argument is aimed at the Irish situation as it was developing with the continued drift away from the Church of Ireland:

> I have never been able to discover, that because an orthodox church was but ill attended by a superstitious people, averse to its doctrines, that could be urged as a sufficient reason why it should be pulled down, especially in places where the inhabitants are numerous. The greater their mental darkness, the greater is their need for gospel light.

His views on Catholicism thus remain much what they were at the time of *Killarney*.

But Patrick Brontë's position was necessarily ambivalent,

and he rallied sharply to any attack on the Irish. In the *Treatise on Baptism*, a reply to the Baptist minister of Hall Green Chapel, Haworth, published in 1836, he invokes the Catholic Church on his side of the argument.

> This church, notwithstanding all its present errors, was once pure: and boasts of higher antiquity than any other church whatsoever. It traces its origin from the time of the apostles. And by tradition and other means, must have a shrewd guess in regard to the best time and mode of Baptism.

What is more, the Baptist minister had evidently irritated Patrick, even in 1836, by attacking the Irish. He replies,

> Do you not know that an Irishman is your lord and master? Are you not under the king's ministry? And are they not under Mr O'Connell, an Irishman? And do not you or your friends pay to him a yearly tribute under the title of rent? And is not the Duke of Wellington, the most famous, and the greatest of living heroes, an Irishman? And dare you, or your adherents, take one political step of importance without trembling, lest it should not meet the approbation of your allies in Ireland? Then as an Irishman might say to you, refrain from your *balderdash* at once, and candidly own your inferiority.

There can be no doubt that the Brontë children read their father's work and were influenced by it. One may argue whether *Wildfell Hall* is directly influenced by *The Maid of Killarney*, or Anne's religious poems by those of her father. However, there is a persistent story that one or other of the daughters checked the proofs. This appears to originate in Scruton's *Thornton and the Brontës*.[7] He quotes a printer from Inkersley's who said that he had seen Charlotte come with her father into Bradford to correct the proofs of a sermon printed in 1824. Gérin considers it more likely that the girl was Maria.[8] Whichever daughter helped her father the story is clear evidence of the family's knowledge of his written work, just as we have already seen evidence that they listened to his stories. If they did read these books and poems, it is hard to escape the view that they noted the Irish flavour in them, though the shift to Killarney instead of Ulster is noticeable in Charlotte's work, and later in her life too, as she travelled on her honeymoon with Arthur Nicholls.

12 *Wuthering Heights*

In an address given at the unveiling of a plaque on Patrick Brontë's birthplace at Imdel in 1956, Dr Phyllis Bentley described the works of the Brontës – presumably thinking in particular of *Wuthering Heights, Jane Eyre* and some poems – as 'a Yorkshire tune played on an Irish harp'. She summed up a feeling many people have when reading these books, and many writers have emphasised the Celtic and Yorkshire mixture. *Wuthering Heights* in particular, 'hewn in a wild workshop' as Charlotte said, exhibits a Yorkshire exterior. But below the surface, is the passion that of German romanticism, the Northern peasantry, or is Emily simply walking 'where my own nature would be leading'? Or are the intuitions of the popular critics correct? Is Emily playing not so much a Yorkshire tune on an Irish harp as an Irish tune on the instruments of Gimmerton brass band?

Any such characterisation runs the risk of over-simplification. Alert and constantly receptive as Emily was, she certainly absorbed the poems and philosophy of Byron, Coleridge and Scott, almost certainly was very influenced by Shelley, and perhaps had in mind the tales of some of the German romantics she had encountered on the continent. But as Ellen Nussey, A. M. F. Robinson and T. Wemyss Reid assert, Emily was a voracious listener to Patrick Brontë's breakfast-time stories, and it was these that 'led her to write *Wuthering Heights*'. It is possible that these writers have overestimated Emily's debt to Patrick's tales; but it looks as if a layer of hunger for and personal commitment to the wild and mythic supernatural, out of which *Wuthering Heights* was formed, set deep in Emily's mind when she was still a child.

Early reviewers compared the novel to Scott, German romance and various other works, including John Banim's *The Nowlans* (1826).[1] Banim and his brother, who wrote under the pseudonym of 'The O'Hara family', produced work on Irish character including sensational or supernatural passages. Other reviewers were at pains to describe the strength of the novel, and several noted its unusual character. While some compared the events and ambience with North English scenes, even at this stage reviewers were quick to see that this was not a social novel in the ordinary meaning of the term.

Looked at from one point of view, *Wuthering Heights* is 'about' family history. Continuity with the past is important. Second and third generations repeat the characteristics of the first, reordering the traits and recombining them. A Cathy will be like Catherine, but not exactly. Linton Heathcliff is part Heathcliff, part Linton, and so on. Hareton, who will carry on the story, is born in 1778, one year after Patrick Brontë, while the main events of the novel take place in 1801–2, the year of Patrick's upheaval, as he vanished from his native land and sailed for Liverpool. (The Gondal saga, too, though we know very little about it, seems to be family history, the story of feuds and civil strife.) Nelly tells much of the story with vividness, recalling the 1770s and 1780s, the days when Patrick Brontë would be a child in Imdel and Ballynaskeagh. Emily, 'Ellis Bell', tells the story with a vividness that suggests she has dwelt in it and changed it organically, as a folk-artist lives his songs and stories. Possibly, through Nelly, Ellis reaches back to Allie or Ellie, in Ireland. (It may appear far-fetched to stress the narrator's name and the author's pseudonym in this way, but oddly similar 'variations on a theme' may be discerned in Emily's Gondal names.) There was an Isabella Linton in Imdel, who married a member of the Glascar meeting, James Stewart, in the late 1790s. She must have been about the same age as Patrick. As neither 'Isabella' nor 'Linton' are Yorkshire names, it seems quite probable that Emily heard her father speak of the girl and was attracted by the name. We may also note the frequence in County Down of the name 'Edgar', regarded there as a surname.

Liverpool is one of the very few real place names in *Wuthering Heights*. It may have been a familiar one to Emily Brontë, for the family were creatures of habit. (One example of this is Patrick Brontë's long-standing preference for the Chapter coffeehouse in London.) Thus Branwell sought the sea at Liverpool years before he saw Scarborough; one of his tasks on his visit of 1839 was to attend the Evangelical church of St Jude to hear the Revd Hugh McNeile, a virulently anti-Catholic Irishman, and bring back an account of his preaching to Patrick Brontë.[2] In the novel, the function of Liverpool seems to be to represent a place known to be real, within walking distance for a healthy man, but through which unusual elements enter the closed Yorkshire world. Such elements cannot quite be naturalised in Yorkshire, though there is an affinity between them and the wind-swept uplands.

Emily Brontë was not compelled to choose Liverpool as the place of entry for her child of storm. She could have chosen Hull, for example, if she wished to imply an overseas descent. Or if she had wished merely to imply an urban and therefore alien background, she could have allowed Heathcliff to be discovered in the streets of Leeds or Sheffield. The choice of Liverpool may well be important. Winifred Gérin points out that Branwell was again in Liverpool in August 1845 and suggests that the form of Heathcliff was influenced by his reports of children newly arrived from Ireland and starving in the city streets.[3] She might well have gone further and reminded us that the starving Irish children were from Patrick's homeland. Welsh, the starving and abandoned child of Hugh's alleged story, also enters upon the scene at Liverpool.

Of course, some of the imaginative ingredients of *Wuthering Heights* come from the narratives told by the Haworth kitchen-servants, especially old Tabby, who is said to have recalled the fairies living in the valley bottoms. Tabby apparently joined the household in 1824, when Emily was six.[4] This was a crucial year for Emily, as her poems show. At about the time when Tabby arrived she was banished to Cowan Bridge for six months. But she must have been listening to stories well before this time, and it is likely that her interest in fairies and the supernatural was well kindled by the time Tabby's stories could have been available to her, on her return from the clergy school in 1825. Unless we distrust Ellen Nussey's account, it seems likely that there was a layer of fairy-lore in Emily's mind before she encountered either Yorkshire folk-tale or the supernatural of Scott and the romantic poets. If the Irish background of the home was strong enough for Charlotte to be speaking with an Irish accent in 1831, it was strong enough for Emily to absorb it before the age of six or seven.

The most basic level of *Wuthering Heights*, then, may have been laid down in Emily's infancy. I have mentioned two aspects of this basic level: family history and the 'stage door' of Liverpool.

But there are other deeply fundamental elements in the book which seem traceable to the early 1820s, Emily's formative years. At this time *The Maid of Killarney*, with its pagan keening over the dead, was Patrick Brontë's latest work. The breakfast-time sessions, including the fairy tales which Emily could repeat 'by the hour together' were in full swing. Mrs Brontë was dead. Over the water, Eilís the never-seen grandmother probably died in 1822, and Maria and Elizabeth were to die in 1825. Death was a central matter in the Brontë household, as it was in some of the 'fairy tales'. Five out of six of our source passages considered these fairy tales to be partly Irish.

In a number of ways, at its deepest level, *Wuthering Heights* bears resemblances to Classic Irish legend or to Anglo-Irish folk tradition. In his assertion that he had heard the outline of the novel before it was published, Wright may not have been thinking of these matters at all; he may have been primarily concerned with the 'story-line' as he perceived it. We shall return to his comment at the end of the chapter. At the moment we shall examine: (i) the pagan, animist nature of the relations between man and nature in the novel; (ii) the intense and amoral nature of 'love' and its capacity to nullify death; and (iii) the oral character of the story, with its Ancient Mariner-like capacity to hypnotise the reader. All these characteristics are to be found in greater or less degree in the Romantics and there is no need to deny their influence on Emily Brontë; yet she gives the impression of concurring with them rather than deriving from them, in that her level of soul-felt intensity appears greater and more constant.

Perhaps the most mysterious place in the area of the Heights is Penistone Crag. The elder Catherine, in delirium, sees Nelly as a hag there:

'I see in you, Nelly,' she continued dreamily, 'an aged woman – you have grey hair, and bent shoulders. This bed is the fairy cave under Penistone Crag, and you are gathering elf-bolts to hurt our heiffers; pretending, while I am there, that they are only locks of wool. That's what you'll come to fifty years hence: I know you are not so now. I'm not wandering, you're mistaken, or else I should believe you really *were* that withered hag, and I should think I *was* under Penistone Crag.'[5]

Penistone Crag, like Liverpool, casts a shadow of place over the Heights. The younger Catherine too is drawn by it as though by the magic of a witch or fairy. Indeed, at Penistone Crag, as at New Grange, there is a fairy cave. The crag and its inhabitants cast a spell on young Catherine which is not referred to afterwards but touches her with supernatural power.

Both English and Irish fairies have harmed cattle with 'elf-shot' in tradition. In Ireland a grey-haired hag called cailleach Vera presided over such pursuits and was imitated by local witches. T. G. F. Paterson gives an example from County Armagh in *Harvest Home*.[6] Emily's folklore is genuine, though it would be impossible to say whether she obtained it from a Yorkshire or an Irish source.

The haunting of the countryside near ' 't Nab' by the ghosts of Heathcliff and 'a woman' near the end of the novel shows mankind, dead or alive, as part of Nature. Country people have met Heathcliff since his death near the church, but town people, of which Lockwood is one, will dismiss such evidence. 'Lockwood's' final comment (or is it Emily Brontë's?) has been the subject of much conjecture and comment. Has the townee become any the wiser for his exposure to the story-telling genius of Nelly, who has striven to lay before him the startling facts of life lived near Nature? Is his calm depiction of the scene at the edge of the churchyard Emily's unequivocal indication that the spirits of Catherine, Edgar Linton and Heathcliff are now at rest? It may be so, but the fluttering of moths among the heath may give us pause, for the notion that butterflies are the souls of the dead is recorded in Lady Wilde's *Ancient Legends, Mystic Charms and Superstitions of Ireland* and in Joseph Ferguson's *Statistical Account of the Parish of Ballymoyer*, though the belief is not confined to Ireland. After mentioning these examples, Wood-Martin says

> In some parts of Ireland the soul is supposed after death to remain in the form of a butterfly, or of a small bird, in the neighbourhood of the body, and then to follow it to the grave.[7]

In an article in *Folklore*, vol. 85 (1974), Dr Jacqueline Simpson lists examples of superstitions used in *Jane Eyre* and *Wuthering Heights*. These include the notion that it is hard to die when birds' feathers have been used for the pillow; that midnight ('the clock striking twelve') is a fatal time to see a ghost or funeral; that a child in a dream indicates bad fortune or death. The first two are referred to in Seán Ó Súilleabháin's *The Types of Irish Folktale*, though it cannot be sure that Emily might not have encountered them or the third one in Yorkshire. Of course, Patrick Brontë's attitude to these legends, if he told them, would be that of Albion in *The Maid of Killarney*: curiosity rather than belief. Emily's attitude reminds us of Hugh Brunty who 'made his listeners see and feel as well as hear'.[8]

Among the other superstitions which Emily may have obtained either from a Yorkshire or an Irish source are the idea that witches run red-hot needles into the feet of their victims; that food should be left on the table at night for fairies to eat; and that a white creature seen at night may be a ghost portending death.[9] The last-mentioned occurs in the scene where Nelly goes to fetch a doctor for Catherine and sees Isabella's spaniel, which Heathcliff has hanged. With this we may compare the activities of the Brontë uncles, using a white sheet to scare their superstitious neighbours in Ballynaskeagh. Such beliefs are widespread in the British Isles and elsewhere. Emily Brontë is quite content to naturalise them in a Yorkshire context, but of their origin we must remain uncertain.

Many European ballads, alive in oral tradition in the eighteenth and nineteenth centuries, see 'love' as an amoral force, producing such positives as cohesion and continuity, even survival after death (though such survival often brings disaster); on the other hand, it also produces jealousy and hate, sometimes in the form of the triangular relationship which leads to murder. Emily Brontë's literary exemplars, such as Coleridge and Shelley, were fully aware of this tradition of course. As well as 'The Ancient Mariner' the Brontës knew 'Christabel', 'John Gilpin', and the poems of Burns, together with many narrative poems of the late eighteenth and early nineteenth centuries which bore a ballad influence. But perhaps this literary tradition is not quite enough to account for Emily's intensely oral style.

As we have seen, Wright credits Patrick Brontë with a number of folk-songs, one of which deals with the vengeance of a betrayed maiden upon her lover. He also mentions the 'Vision of Hell' poem, which seems much nearer to Irish Classic tradition. If the attributions are correct, or if at any rate Patrick Brontë knew and performed these songs, this may be one source of

Emily's ear for folk-song. She does, however, mention in *Wuthering Heights* two ballads which can be recognised. These are 'The Ghaist's Warning' and 'Fairy Annie's Wedding'. J. F. Goodrich considers that the first of these is most likely to have been found in the notes to *The Lady of the Lake*.[10] The second is a puzzle we need to discuss below. The quotation from 'The Ghaist's Warning' is in Scots form, and illustrates the Brontë enthusiasm for all things Scottish which may in part be due to a wish to emphasise the respectable Scots part of their Ulster heritage. This ballad is linked with 'Sweet William's Ghost', a story of a revenant continuing relations with a lover lost through death.

The view of the balladists and their successors seems to be that death will not separate ghost and lover, but that this is not necessarily a good thing. It may be that the lover, by his or her grief, disturbs the peace of the corpse. The corpse will return, sometimes in a form barely recognisable, to the lover's room. Many versions of such ballads and their derivatives are found in the Irish tradition, though they are often supposed to be Scandinavian in origin. In many versions the dead lover cannot stay long, and spends the time persuading the other to relax the grip of affection, so that the corpse can rest. Emily's poetry contains many lovers who retain a yearning affection for the dead person, and it is hard not to see this as a matter Emily faced within herself, as she contemplated the death and separation of her mother, Maria and Elizabeth. Lockwood's intense vision of Catherine as a child-ghost seems to the point here, since it is not quite in all ways appropriate to the plot that the dream should be presented as a ghost at this point in the story: yet this 'nightmare' seems very like a ghost.

There is no known ballad called 'Fairy Annie's Wedding'. It is possible that the title may represent a confusion in Emily's mind. Two ballads have versions in which a girl called Fair Annie appears. These are numbers 62 and 74 in Child's *The English and Scottish Popular Ballads*.[11] There appears to be a connection between the two, and both have themes which occur in *Wuthering Heights*. 'Fair Annie' (no. 62) tells of a girl stolen by a knight in her childhood and later bearing a number of children to him. She is replaced by a legitimate wife, whom she must welcome as a bride to the household. She plays her part well, but at night retires to mourn. The bride hears her complaints and discovers her story, then leaves the knight and Fair Annie, returning to her own home beyond the seas. Child prints a partial version from County Meath, and other Irish versions have been collected since.[12]

In 'Sweet William and Fair Annie' (no. 74), William courts the fair-haired Annie, but decides to marry the 'brown girl' for her houses and land. He bids Annie to the wedding, where there is an angry exchange between the girls. In most versions the brown girl attacks Annie and kills her, only to be viciously killed in her turn by William (or Lord Thomas, as he more often becomes). Child collected a version of this ballad in Killarney, and many versions have since been collected in Ireland as well as Scotland and England.

It will be seen that either of these two ballads might have been called 'Fair Annie's Wedding', since in both the crucial point is the wedding of a usurper to Annie's true love at a marriage which should have been hers. The second of the two introduces Emily Brontë's favourite opposition (found in the poems as well as the novel) of dark-haired to light-haired. It will be recalled that 'Welsh', in Wright's version of Hugh's alleged story, is persistently dark, while the Brontës, exemplified by the aunts and Eilís McClory, are light. Of course, in *Wuthering Heights* the triangle is stood on its head. It is Catherine who has a choice between light-haired socially respectable Edgar and dark-haired outcast Heathcliff. But it does seem possible that some version or other of this ballad lurked below the surface of Emily's consciousness and became one source of the book.

However, the title of the song as given by Nelly is '*Fairy* Annie's Wedding'. No version in Child suggests a supernatural origin for Annie, but it may possibly be that the heroine has become confused with the Irish goddess Anna or Ania, whose memory lingered on in folklore for centuries after Christianity had replaced her. Nelly's comment that the ballad 'goes to a dance' for all its sadness is typical of the known versions of the ballad, and indeed many ballads with sad words use lively tunes. Emily had apparently heard this ballad sung, whether in the Haworth kitchen or by Patrick, or by James Brontë on his visit about 1846. As *Fairy* Annie was the heroine, we may think it possible that this was one of the 'fairy' tales which Emily repeated 'by the hour' in her childhood.

Though I have cited versions of both the ballads in *Wuthering Heights* from Ireland, it is right to say that Child did not draw many of his examples from there. In fact, the ballad tradition seems to have been relatively weak in most counties of Ireland, as appears from work done by Hugh Shields, the Irish folk-song collector.[13] The Gælic tradition favours prose for narrative and verse for lyric. However, ballads were invading Ireland from Britain at least as early as plantation times. Some were translated into Irish while many waited for acceptance until English became the dominant language. Thus it is hard to see these narratives becoming well known in County Down before Hugh Brunty's generation, though we have the ascription of the folk-songs in the following generation as indications that such words and stories would be well known by the beginning of the nineteenth century. Hugh Shields does, however, list both the ballads we have considered likely to have influenced *Wuthering Heights* among a very limited list of ballads he has traced in Ireland.

Folk-ballads are, of course, only one example of oral narrative art. In previous pages I have argued that such hints as Wright gives of the content of Hugh Brunty's stories suggest that he was a seanchaí, with both some of the old hero-legends and some more modern legends in his repertoire. If Hugh could write Irish from childhood (and he may have been taken from his 'comfortable home' too early for this) he is considered largely illiterate on his arrival in the neighbourhood of Donaghmore. On the other hand, his oral technique, according to the accounts Wright heard, partook of the stock-in-trade of the Gælic storyteller of whom Seamus Delargey wrote.[14]

Patrick's art too was often oral. He frightened his breakfast-time guests, wove webs of words in the pulpit 'with nothin'' in his hand' and even in old age entertained Mrs Gaskell with his voluble charm and courtesy. Though Mr Brontë had enormous reverence for the book, which he passed on to all his children, the whole family listened acutely. The conversation recorded on the 1837 diary paper is a good example of this, with words accurately written so that as we read it we can imagine the conversation between Emily and Anne. Listening and telling were in the family. Paper was sometimes merely a means of recording the spoken word, not a fresh medium. Hence Nelly, who gives little away about herself throughout the novel, still seems intensely real. The origin of this oral alertness is the Irish story-telling tradition of Hugh and perhaps Pádraig Ó Pronntaigh.

But very little of the matters we have considered sprang to the mind of the lively but unliterary Wright on first reading *Wuthering Heights*. 'I read the Brontë novels with the feeling that I had already known what was coming', he says.[15] It was the story-line that Wright thought he knew. It might be valuable at this point to discuss the similarities between what Emily actually wrote and what Wright had heard from the old men who remembered Hugh Brunty.

Many things are dissimilar. The rivalry in love between the old farmer Burns and Hugh Brunty for the hand of Eilís bears no relation at all to the rivalry between Heathcliff and Edgar Linton. The outcome is also quite different, and the runaway marriage has no parallel except with the escapade after which Heathcliff marries Isabella. The major theme of the dead lover holding the attention of the live has no trace in *The Brontës in Ireland*: all Wright's ghosts are trivial ones. The Boyne farm is a deserted ruin, while Wuthering Heights is at least habitable. The ironic parallel of the second generation does not occur in Wright's story, while in the novel it is vital. It begins to seem far-fetched to compare the story of Hugh Brunty with *Wuthering Heights* at all.

But, of course, the element that Wright thought he recognised was the identity of Heathcliff and Welsh. The latter appears, like Heathcliff, in the vicinity of Liverpool. He is adopted for no good reason except perhaps that of charity, but he worms his way into the family like a changeling and soon becomes his adopted parents' mainstay. He schemes until he wins the property, just like Heathcliff. He then warps the character of the genuine heir in the next generation; we may compare Hareton with Hugh Brunty. Ill-treatment is his constant delight, though he is not considered to be literally a tool of the devil as is sometimes hinted of Heathcliff. But he is the perpetual alien, throwing the house out of its destiny. He has gained his influence through an almost incestuous marriage with a foster-sister (in the novel, this marriage remains a matter of the soul).

It may be worth noting that Heathcliff has only one name which does for both Christian and surname. He is said to be named after a child of the old Earnshaws but he is never called Heathcliff Earnshaw in the book and the singularity of his name increases his oddness. Welsh, too, possesses only one name, said to be a nickname descriptive of his looks and origin. In Wright's narrative he is always called Welsh, though at one point he is said to have assumed the name Brontë. He is depicted as wily, violent and passionate, but like Heathcliff he is capable of gentlemanly behaviour. It is odd that Emily Brontë simply tells us of Heathcliff's three-year absence and never explains or hints where he has been. At this point it almost does seem as if she is following an exemplar and has no interest in the side-issue.

In both stories the ancestral hall collapses under the influence of the cuckoo, though the Boyne house is much worse. The motif of the house in collapse is found in Emily's poems too, and the wild orphan persists throughout her work until the last lengthy fragment of 1846. When Wright describes his feeling that he had read *Wuthering Heights* before, it may have been the orphan story he had particularly in mind. Indeed, this is the element in *Jane Eyre* which McKee is supposed to have seized upon.

Wright was no literary critic. His reaction to *Wuthering Heights* was spontaneous. The orphan story is the part of the Hugh Brunty legend which corresponds most clearly with *Wuthering Heights*. As I have suggested earlier in this chapter, there is reason to believe it possible that other aspects of the novel have an Irish, or at least a ballad, origin; but it is the orphan story and the story of the orphan's vengeance which bears the closest similarity to the dark legend from eighteenth-century Ireland. It is hard to see how William Wright's identification of this element with the legend of Hugh Brunty which his first Classical teacher made him write in various versions could have no basis whatever in reality.

13 Lyric Poems and Rebellion in Gondal

Emily Brontë's poetry, like *Wuthering Heights*, shows some signs of having developed out of the considerations which fixed her attention in childhood. We may begin by turning to one of the few Irish commentators on the Irish elements in the Brontës' work. Cathal O'Byrne wrote his *The Gælic Source of the Brontë Genius* in 1933.[1] He takes a great deal of Wright's work at its face value, but he also looks at the extracts copied by Pádraig Ó Pronntaigh and quoted by Hyde in *The Story of Early Gælic Literature*, a forerunner to *A Literary History of Ireland* which has already been mentioned. He compares some third-century work ascribed to Finn McCumhail, in which there is a bright description of a spring day, with the well-known passage in *Wuthering Heights* in which Catherine and Linton argue about motion or rest as ways of spending warm days on the moors.

He considers that one poem of Emily's has 'the true Gælic cadence' and quotes

> On a sunny bræ alone I lay
> One summer afternoon.
> It was the marriage time of May
> With her young lover June.[2]

This poem does have an internal rhyme, common in Irish folk-song, but also in Emily's romantic exemplars. It is a little unlike other poems by Emily, and a product of her late, sceptical period. In it, the poet holds a dialogue with her soul, uniquely for Emily Brontë, though there are many poems by both Emily and Anne in which various forms of internal dialogue occur. The poem is not one chosen to represent Emily in *The Oxford Book of Irish Verse*, but it does have an airy feeling, accentuated by the short lines as well as the internal rhyme. In its later stages, however, the thought of the poem seems traceable to Shelley.

The problem about ascribing this kind of direct Gælic influence to Emily Brontë's poetry is that it is difficult to see how it could have been mediated. It is virtually certain that Hugh Brunty spoke Irish and knew some Gælic poetry, just as he knew Gælic legends. Patrick may have spoken some Irish, as witness his understanding of the old women at the wake; but that he repeated much Irish poetry to his uncomprehending children seems unlikely. It seems more likely that Celtic echoes should be ascribed to second-hand sources such as Scott, Ossian, Burns and Hogg.

But if we regretfully set aside the possibility that Emily could have been influenced by Gælic poetry in its pure state, there is certainly no need to discount folk influences on her, or on Anne. The richness of the folk-artistic background of the Irish Brontës has by now been established in these pages, and to suppose that none of this penetrated to the children is most improbable. We might draw a parallel with John Clare, whose father was a noted fiddler and ballad singer, and who himself collected ballads in his youth. These ballads permeate his poems, and their influence is detectable, intermingled with the eighteenth-century mentors in which he soaked himself. Likewise Emily and Anne Brontë approach folk rhythms on many occasions, though their poetry also grows out of eighteenth-century writers such as Cowper, hymnologists, and the Romantics such as Wordsworth and Coleridge, whose 'ballad-metre' poems merge their effect with the folk-material.

Even Anne Brontë's early poems are divested of superfluous adjectives and give the impression of very bare workmanship. However, in 'The Bluebell' of 22 August 1840, she produces a line direct from folk-song:

> That day along a sunny road
> *All carelessly I strayed. . . .*

Compare with this, from 'The Banks of Claudy'

> As I walked out one morning
> All in the month of May
> Down through some flower gardens
> *So carelessly did stray. . . .* [3]

The formula is not from Wordsworth, Coleridge, or a literary balladist. 'The Banks of Claudy', though naturalised in England, is agreed to be of Irish origin.

There are many examples of folk-style in Emily's verse. An example which appears to quote directly from a ballad is 'Loud without the wind was roaring' of November 1838. The quotations are described as 'Wild words of an ancient song', and are 'It was spring, for the skylark was singing', and 'It was morning; the bright sun was beaming'.[4] These formulæ could fit the opening of many folk-songs, but I have suggested that the most probable may be a version of 'Reynardine', of which George Sigerson wrote a version beginning

> The morn was breaking bright and fair
> The lark sang in the sky. . . .

The song concerns the life of an outlaw 'On the mountains of Pomeroy' in Sigerson's version, though there is no suggestion that this particular version could have been known to Patrick Brontë, since Sigerson was not born until 1838. The place of Sigerson's birth, Strabane in Ulster, may be significant.

It may be that the use of the name Ula for an island in the Gondal complex does not echo the Irish word Uladh (pronounced without the final consonant) which means 'Ulster'.[5] However, it is interesting that Emily several times introduces into her Gondal verse a character called 'Iernë', the only possible meaning of which could be 'The Irish girl', though the spelling is not itself Gælic.[6] In one poem, the girl seems to be a personification of Emily herself, sitting up during the small hours of the morning and hearing the chimes of the clock nearby: a fictional metamorphosis of the Haworth church chimes. In another poem Iernë holds a conversation with her father in which she laments their isolation in prison, but maintains that the dead know no such lamentation in their happier position on high. Again, there is a degree of self-identification with Iernë, and the close relationship between the girl and her father is worth noting.

Perhaps the most interesting self-identification of Emily Brontë's is Geraldine, the imperious and wicked princess of Gondal, whose heartless adultery and murder at times makes Gondal seem totally unreal.[7] I have elsewhere suggested that Emily may have found the name in 'Christabel', and been attracted by this portrayal of a sinister dark 'twin', since she herself at times considered that she stood in this type of relationship with Anne. In this choice, Emily may not have been guided by the Irish origin of the name, yet she could have learned, for example in Moore's *History of Ireland*, of the heroic and romantic doings of the Geraldine clan during the middle ages. It would not be too far fetched to see in the character of Geraldine Emily's tribute to all the naked wildness of Ireland which she felt had been sacrificed in the family's adoption into the regulated world of the English bourgeoisie.

Details have been given in an earlier chapter of the escapades of William Brontë, Patrick's closest brother, during the rebellion of 1798. Patrick himself did not take an active part in the rebellion, which took place during the final period of his teaching at Glascar. However, I have made it clear that the main thrust of the uprising in Ulster was no more Catholic than Presbyterian. Many Presbyterian clergy supported the movement, and it may be that Patrick could hear a favourable opinion of the rebels both at home from his Catholic cousins, and at the meeting-house from the Presbyterians. As we have seen, the details of the action at Ballynahinch were handed down from William to later generations, and it is hard to suppose that no reference to 1798, the most exciting year of his life in Ireland, would be passed on by Patrick to his children during one of the breakfast-time storysessions.

We may also recall that in *The Maid of Killarney* Patrick Brontë is willing to state a radical case for legal reform. *The Maid of Killarney* was written when Charlotte was three and the older children no more than five or six. It seems possible that an early childhood memory of the Brontë children may have been Patrick's impassioned talk of legal reform, and the mysterious stories he told of their uncle William's personal involvement in a political cause. Certainly Patrick gradually became less forcefully attracted to such causes, and became a Tory, but during his children's infancy they might well have heard of both the excitement and the moral righteousness of civil war.

We shall shortly be exploring the matter of civil war in the Gondal writings of Emily and Anne. First, it will be worth restating some of the events of 1798 as seen by the Brontë family of County Down, by William and by Patrick. Wright tells us that after the battle William was 'pursued by the cavalry, who fired at him repeatedly, but he led them into a bog and escaped'.[8] We have already seen John Brontë's own version of this. Wright says that after the battle, 'the Welsh Horse' devastated the country far and wide. They arrived at Hugh Brunty's house at Ballynaskeagh and set light to the thatch, 'after a short parley with his wife, in which neither understood the other'. It was on this occasion that Hugh is supposed to have spoken to the soldiers in Irish, whereupon they doused the flames.

Thus Hugh Brunty's house was saved despite what Wright calls his 'advanced and disloyal views'.

An excellent account of the 1798 rebellion in County Down is to be found in McComb's *Guide to Belfast* of 1861. It is too long and detailed to quote here, but the stirring events in which Henry Munro's citizen army were involved might well have a great effect on their relatives and neighbours, when they reached home and told their tale. In all there were 7000 men, who gathered together on 11 June at Windmill Hill in Ballynahinch. Munro was the soul of honour, who would not allow misbehaviour among his men. He scorned to attack the enemy at night. Once the army had been engaged and defeated, there were the usual stories of betrayal, and Munro was executed, his head being stuck up on a pillar at Lisburn after his death.[9]

Whether or not we agree entirely with Miss Fannie Ratchford's reconstruction of the Gondal saga, it is clear that a strong element in it is the fight between loyalists and rebels. In Emily's diary paper of 1845, and in other places, it is made evident that the fight is between Royalists and the attacking Republicans by whom they are 'hard driven'. In Anne's poem 'Z's dream', of 14 September 1846, we have the lament of a man who has killed his friend in civil war, and if we go back a year to the same summer as the diary paper, we find in Anne's 'Song', of 4 September 1845, a joyful pæan in praise of victory: 'The Tyrants are o'er thrown; the land is free!' But as the poem continues, the speaker is overcome with the sadness that freedom has to be bought with the death of men who were once seen as 'tyrants' but are now 'victims'.[10]

Emily began her final poem in September 1846, at about the same date as Anne's lament mentioned above.[11] It was never to be finished, but its theme is clear. Although in the Gondal tradition it conceals its location: 'Why ask to know the date, the clime?' A wanderer or mercenary has arrived in a foreign land. He is very much alone, and though he has senior officers to whom he is responsible, he finds himself out of sympathy with the cause he has espoused. He sees in his mind's eye the 'wood-shadowed dales' in which are blackened stones, 'Self-piled in cairns o'er burning bones'. A stark and unromantic picture of a ruined and burning city is painted; it is 'Smoke-hidden in the winding glen'. (Emily Brontë's unselfconscious use of the Irish 'glen' is frequent.)

The geography of the country where the war is fought is much like County Down, though, of course, it is not unlike Yorkshire. As has been said, this land is unnamed; it is 'that land of woe'. As Patrick Brontë says in his letter to Hugh ten years later, in 1858,

> If they would in Ireland leave off their Bible burning, murdering and quarrelling with each other ... Ireland, instead of being a degraded country, would be one of the most respectable portions of the globe.[12]

The land in Emily's last poem is not Gondal, at least not by name. It will be recalled that James Brontë visited Haworth, probably in 1846. It seems possible that his visit stirred memories of the origins, in childhood, of the sisters' interest in rebellion and its excitement. By 1846, they may well have been seeing the consequences of rebellion reflected in the devastation of the potato famine.

William Brontë escaped across high ground towards County Armagh. Anne allows her rebels to 'range the mountains wild'. The rebel army in 1798 marched with various emblems: hats and button-holes decorated with laurel, green or yellow belts, a harp entwined with shamrock or bays ('but without the crown'), while the regular soldiers of the army fought under their usual colours.

> One race, beneath two standards, fighting
> For Loyalty and Liberty,

says Emily Brontë of the two armies in her final poem. Like the city in her poem, Ballynahinch was burnt.

The King's troops entered it early in the night, as it was then deserted by the other party, and it was plundered by them of everything valuable. They then set it on fire: 63 houses were burned: 69, including the houses of worship, were left standing; but all were pillaged of everything that was valuable in them, and wrecked.[13]

It may have been the echo of the 1798 rebellion that caused Emily to write 'When kindred strive – God help the weak!', although it is quite likely that feelings and events in Haworth parsonage may have added poignancy to such a reflection.

In many other poems Emily sympathises with the outlaw, ejected from his rightful place by rebels, or with the rebels themselves, justifiably attacking a corrupt aristocracy. As has been said, Patrick Brontë's own position gradually developed to that of a reluctant but not bigoted Tory, upholding after his Cambridge initiation the system of Church and State and passing on to Charlotte the rather snobbish respect he had acquired for his betters. But the undercurrent of Irish patriotism which was still strong in his early days at Haworth fascinated Emily and Branwell more than the surface of respectable Toryism. Emily allows her tyrants to glory in their ruthless deeds, but, especially in these later poems, she records the feelings of escapers and stragglers, exiles on the rough moors. Her tone is very similar to what we learn of uncle William, pursued by the cavalry away from Ballynahinch.

Of course, Scott's influence is detected in all this. But Scott's wilder scenes were being read by children already conversant with the outlaw's life. The Gælic names which find their way into Gondal are partly from Scott, no doubt. Roderic, Douglas, Gleneden and Una with Lucia MacElgin are found in the sisters' Gondal works. But incidentally, Una's surname is Campbell, the surname of their uncle Welsh's wife. No doubt the Celtic and romantic names of Scott were strengthened by the children's reading of such writers as Moore, whose *History of Ireland* has already been mentioned. Emily's hero Shelley had written passionately about Irish politics, and we may also recall the Irish patriotism of Swift, whose *Gulliver's Travels* the young Brontës enjoyed and often recalled. It is perhaps worth noting that Wellington, Swift and Moore were *respectable* Irishmen, like Patrick Brontë. But their respectability had not cut them off from their homeland with which, like Patrick Brontë they maintained a passionate love–hate relationship.

Before leaving the matter of names of Irish origin, we may mention the odd circumstance that Gilbert Markham in *The Tenant of Wildfell Hall* has a brother named Fergus who growls, sulks and at times exhibits the wilder (both in a pleasant and unpleasant sense) traits of Branwell. Branwell's other name, Patrick, by which he was known in the village, was a constant reminder to the Brontë sisters of their disreputable Irishness, and Anne must surely have chosen Fergus' name wittingly, to emphasise his character; there is no evidence that Fergus had become a popular name among the Yorkshire farmers of the time, and in fact Anne's story relates supposedly to the 1820s. It seems most probable that she adopted the name from Feargus O'Connor, the Chartist leader. But the nuances of the name cut both ways: Anne wishes to suggest a lighthearted and irresponsible tease, but by her very choice of the name and sympathy with its bearer she underlines her comment to James Brontë that she wished to go 'home' with him.

14 Charlotte's Irish Accent

It may perhaps be said that Charlotte Brontë's attitude to Ireland always partook of suspicion, hostility and embarrassment. Most commentators have noted the irony that is present in the situation of an authoress who mocks Irish clergy in *Shirley* and ends up by marrying an Irish curate. However, we see a development from the juvenile writings to the mature work. In *Jane Eyre* and *Shirley* Ireland is remote and uncivilised, but though these characteristics form a part of Charlotte's attitude in childhood, they are dominated at that time by the romantic and martial elements in Ireland: we do not forget Charlotte's hero-worship of the Duke of Wellington, an Irish nobleman most dear to the hearts of all the family.

Two short works dating from 1829, when Charlotte was thirteen, may illustrate this earlier viewpoint. *An Adventure in Ireland* is dated 29 April 1829. Set in a southern woodland in which there are mountains, villages and castles, the story concerns a traveller who takes up the offer of a night's lodging in the castle of a certain Mr O'Callaghan. He is shown to his room in a turret by a boy called Dennis Mulready, whose name (not found in County Down) is gratuitously inserted though he has little part to play in the story. It looks as if the name was given purely because of the romantic sound of Irish names. The same may be true of the place names Cahin and Killala in this story. However, it may be worth noting that Killala made history once, when the French forces landed there during the 1798 uprising in which Charlotte's uncle William took a minor part. Just possibly the name of this remote western village had been mentioned by Patrick Brontë while recounting the tale of the rebellion during breakfast time.

Mulready tells the traveller that 'they say that the ould master's ghost has been sitting on that there chair', and that he can be heard washing his hands in the basin 'often and often'. (The significance of this hand-washing is not explained and presumably suggests guilt on the part of the ghost.) The traveller lies down in fear and sleeps fitfully. After about an hour he wakes to find 'looking through my curtains a skeleton wrapped in a white sheet'. The use of a white sheet to represent a ghost, in conjunction with candles, on the part of the Brontë uncles, has already been mentioned. On returning to sleep the traveller dreams, and his dreams are influenced by the windy night, as appears when Dennis Mulready comes to wake him up and tells him about the night's weather.

In August of the same year Charlotte wrote *The Search after Happiness*, the hero of which is one Henry O Donell. Much of the story takes place in Africa, and the plot appears to be linked with Glasstown by the inclusion of Wellington and the Marquis of Douro. The eastern aura of the book owes a great deal to *The Arabian Nights*, but the Irish choice of name for the hero may not be without significance. He is said to be a 'nobleman of great consequence' and we note that 'his mind was strong and unbending, his disposition unsociable and though respected by many he was loved by few'. He shows himself during the piece to be a martially minded adventurer, and he provides Charlotte with an interesting self-identification.

In these two tales we see that at this point Charlotte considered the Irish valiant, adventurous, romantic and superstitious. She likes the sound of Irish names, and exaggerates the beauty of Irish country, but is careful to locate her Irish castle in 'the south of Ireland', not Ulster. We recall Patrick Brontë's information to Mrs Gaskell that Hugh Brunty came 'from the south' and his hint of wealth in an earlier generation. There is certainly little in the account of Ireland which may emanate from Patrick, though possibly Dennis Mulready's pronunciation of 'old' may be more northern than southern. However, Charlotte does seem clear that Ireland is the place to find ghosts, and she seems to know what they are likely to look like. The reference adds weight to Ellen Nussey's descriptions of Patrick's breakfast-time story-telling.

In *An Adventure in Ireland* Charlotte sees herself as a (possibly English) traveller, and her view of Ireland is external. By her use of the name O Donell for her hero in *The Search after Happiness* she creates a much closer link for herself, though nowhere is O Donell's nationality mentioned.

As has already been said, it is possible that the 'fortune-telling' incident in *Jane Eyre* had been suggested by James

Brontë's escapade in County Down. There is obviously no manner in which such an influence could be proved, especially in view of the uncertainty surrounding the precise date at which James visited Haworth. The other Irish episode in *Jane Eyre* is much more in line with Patrick Brontë's *Maid of Killarney* and the earlier examples of Charlotte's writing which we have just examined. Mrs Dionysius O'Gall verges on the stage-Irish.

It will be remembered that when Rochester is apparently considering a wedding with Blanche, he suggests that Jane and Adèle should leave. He mentions a post which he might be able to secure for Jane, teaching the 'five daughters' of Mrs O'Gall, whose address is Bitternutt Lodge, Connaught. 'You'll like Ireland', he drily remarks, 'They're such warm-hearted people there, they say.' Not only are the proper names chosen to deny the implication of this, but Rochester admits, 'I never go over to Ireland, not having myself much of a fancy for the country.' His remarks exemplify an attitude to Ireland which we shall see repeated in *Shirley*.

Like *Killarney* and *An Adventure in Ireland*, the passage refers to the South. It seems that Charlotte, following her father, is avoiding any direct reference to Ulster. This interesting evasion can be explained, perhaps, by supposing that her North Irish ancestry was too painful a matter to be directly touched on, but that it could be repudiated by implication in her attacks on the Southern Irish. Irish warm-heartedness is mentioned here ironically: gall and bitterness appear to be the more natural associations felt by Jane and Rochester. We may perhaps think it possible that to mention Irish ancestry was for Charlotte to touch a raw nerve, associated with bitter feelings.

It was not, however, to the passage about Mrs O'Gall that David McKee was referring when he read *Jane Eyre* in Ballynaskeagh manse, perhaps in 1853, and was struck by its coherence with Brontë family tradition. Wright gives two accounts of the first Irish reading of *Jane Eyre*, the first a short one in chapter II, in which after a reading *en famille* of the book handed to McKee by Hugh, McKee finally rises and says, 'That is the greatest novel that has been written in my time; but it is Brontë all over from beginning to end.' In the second version, in chapter XXVIII of *The Brontës in Ireland*, we read that the Brontë family tried to read the 'three volumes of babble' for themselves, but finally laid down the work in despair. At this point Hugh 'tied up the three volumes in a red handkerchief' and took them to Mr McKee.¹

Recalling that Wright's future wife was present at the interview, we can allow a certain amount of credence to his account. Hugh arrived at McKee's manse about teatime and 'began in a low, mysterious whisper' to talk about *Jane Eyre* as though his niece had been guilty of an indiscretion. We remember that James Brontë had brought back a most unflattering picture of Charlotte, and that this might suggest that little was to be expected of her. McKee then read 'the book' (as Wright puts it, forgetting that at the beginning of his account he had insisted on the three-volume nature of the work), and was captivated by it. His words, as given in chapter XXVIII, are a second version of the judgement given in chapter II:

> Hughey ... the book bears the Brontë stamp on every sentence and idea, and it is the grandest novel that has been produced in my time. ... The child Jane Eyre is your father in petticoats, and Mrs Reed is the wicked uncle by the Boyne.²

It is such 'doublets' as these two versions of McKee's speech which show us Wright's method, accurate in essentials, careless in detail.

As in the case of *Wuthering Heights* it is absurd to suppose that the Haworth Brontës consciously obtained their stories from their Irish ancestry, yet McKee's first impressions are of interest. What elements did McKee recognise immediately as stemming from that ancestry?

The prevalence of the orphan theme, so evident in much Brontë writing, could be explained if all or part of the story of Welsh, or of Hugh Brunty, was known to them. McKee's underlying perception here is that the status of orphan is of maximal interest to Charlotte as well as Emily, and that the depth at which the theme runs in the books is not explicable by reference to the loss by the children of their own mother at an early age. In McKee's second alleged gloss, not reported in Wright's chapter II, we have the equation between Hugh Brunty and Jane Eyre. As Hugh escapes from his hated place of adoption, so does Jane. As Jane reacts passionately to injustice, so according to legend did Hugh Brunty. Their reaction to institutional religion seems similar: Jane is repelled by Brocklehurst and unwilling to see marriage to St John Rivers as her duty. Hugh's detachment from both Catholic and Protestant faiths seems attested however one interprets the alleged events of his wedding preparations.

Like *Wuthering Heights*, *Jane Eyre* assumes a background of Gothic feeling which it is easy to ascribe totally to the reading of the girls in the works of Mrs Shelley and others. Doubtless such an ascription is partly correct. McKee sees a more primitive level in the supernatural elements of *Jane Eyre*, which echo (not without irony) the popular superstitious beliefs in country places in such a way as to suggest to the reader a deep interest in such supernatural events even while they are being derided by the author. Thus the Brontë uncles dress up, hold turnip-lanterns to the faces of their victims, set the glen on fire for a joke, and make strange noises echo from the hills, to create in fun an air of mystery not radically different from that created by Charlotte as she plans the important part to be played in the novel by spectral dogs, ghostly noises at night, Fuseli-like effects of candlelight falling upon the hideous face of Bertha, and so on. Charlotte is using these effects in a sophisticated literary way, but her irony matches interestingly the irony of her uncles in Ballynaskeagh.

It is not here asserted that Charlotte Brontë is consciously making use of attitudes or stories taken in from the narration of her father or from other members of the family on their rare visits to Yorkshire. This seems likely to be far from the truth, her general distrust of Irishness suggesting that she would have repudiated such influences. The individualism of Jane Eyre, however, does seem to portray a family trait, both in the Brontës of Haworth and those of Ulster. David McKee apparently recognised this parallel in his remarks to Hugh the younger. As to the final alleged sentence of the second version of his remarks, we must suspend judgement. He may have said, 'Mrs Reed is the wicked uncle by the Boyne', but there is little detailed comparison between the character of Mrs Reed and Welsh, and no comparison at all in their circumstances. It is most likely that, apart from the bare notion of the wicked aunt, Charlotte discovered the elements of Mrs Reed's character and situation elsewhere.

A good deal more reference to Irishness is made in *Shirley*, particularly through the character and adventures of Mr Malone, said to be based on James William Smith, who became curate to Mr Brontë in 1842, moved to Keighley in 1844, and eventually left for Canada in 1847 leaving sundry debts and a bad reputation.³ Malone has a 'genuinely national' face, consisting of 'the high-featured, North-American-Indian sort of visage, which belongs to a certain class of the Irish gentry'. Mr Malone is said to be 'besottedly arrogant'. Charlotte's view of a typical Irish gentleman is not a flattering one.

By now, however, there do seem to be ways in which Charlotte is meeting the feeling of inferiority resulting from her Irish descent more courageously, for she allows Malone some characteristics of her father. He is said to carry loaded pistols in his pockets, and to take a shillelagh with him on his pastoral visits, as Patrick Brontë did at Hartshead. Small boys run behind him shouting 'Irish Peter!' as small boys had teased Patrick Brontë and called him 'Papish Pat'. The sound of his voice is described: he pronounces 'firm', 'helm' and 'storm' with an extra vowel, and his intonation is said to be 'high' and 'Celtic'.⁴ Commentators noted that Partick Brontë's voice was 'musical', though as we have seen they claimed to detect a Scottish rather than an Irish pronunciation.

Nevertheless, Charlotte still wishes to ascribe her typical Irishman to Connaught rather than Ulster. Mr Helstone upbraids Malone fiercely:

> I wish when you had crossed the Channel, you had left your Irish ways behind you. Dublin student ways won't do here: the proceedings which might pass unnoticed in a wild bog and mountain district in Connaught will, in a decent English parish, bring disgrace on those who indulge in them.⁵

Malone is a drinker, and quarrelsome; he is also a gallant where ladies are concerned. His character is well shown when in chapter XVI he brings roses for Shirley just when she is in the mood to create a 'scene'. Shirley cannot forbear to smile, and instantly Malone's romance changes to hatred. None of the curates are taken seriously by their creator, but Malone is perhaps the one from whose foibles the greatest degree of mirth is extracted. There is certainly very little attempt by Charlotte to give a subjective or sympathetic view of Malone. Despite the characteristics he shares with her father, he is seen externally, as a changeable and irrational man, whose habits, speech and appearance make him a figure of fun.

Finally, of course, Charlotte amazed herself and affronted her father by accepting the offer of marriage made by Arthur Bell Nicholls, an Irish curate. The utter and implacable opposition of Patrick Brontë to their marriage seems likely to have been based on two principal grounds.[6] First, he had no wish for Charlotte to return to a society whose stigma he had outgrown and from which he had successfully protected his daughters since their childhood, though Branwell had succumbed to some very Irish excesses. Secondly, he may well have thought that Mr Nicholls would have sufficient knowledge of society in Ireland to be able to unearth some of the disreputable facts he had buried away from his circle of acquaintance in England, and from his own children in their maturity, except when ugly traces of these facts were unearthed at such times as the visit of uncle James in 1846: Catholicism, rebelliousness, superstition and the 'gibberish' of the Irish language. Mr Nicholls 'generally sees your letters', he writes to Hugh in 1858: possibly meaning 'be careful what you say; do not let too much of the "wild" Irish show in what you write'.

It is not part of my intention to deal with Charlotte's relations with Nicholls once her father relented, or with their Irish honeymoon. It is worth noting that they kept well away from Ulster though both had relations there, Mr Nicholls' of a somewhat higher social rank than Charlotte's. Charlotte writes in a letter with surprise of the 'English order and repose' she finds at Banagher when she arrives with her new husband. Clearly, the impression of Ireland received from her father was of chaos and 'Irish negligence'. At Banagher we must leave her, returned to the land of her ancestry, safe in the home of a scion of the Scots–Irish ascendancy and in extremely different surroundings from the tiny cottage where her father had been born so many years before.

We have reached the end of this exploration. There are still many points where certainty has not been reached, points which may be settled by further searches in the remaining manuscript records of eighteenth-century Ireland. But during the course of this book we have found evidence that Patrick Brontë did convey to his children at least a flavour of Irish tradition. The sheer *orality* of *Wuthering Heights*, for example, shows that Emily retained the gift of her grandfather, the seanchaí. He had been brought up as an Irish speaker, but could certainly hold his Presbyterian neighbours spellbound as he roasted the corn at the corn-kiln. His material was a mixture of local ghost stories, hero-legends of the Classic tradition, ballads, his own life-history, and political/religious theory. Fire looms large in the corn-kiln. The baby Patrick feared it ever afterwards. Emily and Charlotte used it prominently in *Wuthering Heights* and *Jane Eyre*. Patrick shook the dust of Ireland off his feet, but his wild eyes and 'cold' smile helped to re-create the long-remembered tales of Irish horror.

We have found that all the Brontë descendants agreed that the seanchaí, Hugh, had been brought up near Drogheda. Alice, Patrick's sister, whose memory stretched back the longest, agreed that he had been taken from his own home and adopted, but that when his place was taken by a new-born sister, he had left and never returned to the Boyne valley. We saw that the Drogheda area was steeped in remote legend, all told in Irish. Everywhere in the place where Hugh grew up were visual reminders of the heroic past, when Aengus Óg, himself a tricky customer, had walked the earth. Now his descendants had become the sídhe, the fairy folk, and lived in Aengus' tomb, which the people called a fairy cave.

Whether Welsh was really discovered on a Liverpool boat is dubious, but J. B. Lusk was convinced that Hugh believed so, and told his story. There seem to be too many similarities between Welsh's story and *Wuthering Heights* for them to be coincidental, and we have an image of little Emily, listening patiently to her father, apparently so that she can collect the whole story. But Wright certainly did not write out pages of the novel before it was published. I have hypothesised that the changeling legend may have covered an illegitimate birth, and suggested a possible local family who may have had some relations with a member of the Brunty or Ó Pronntaigh clan. It would be foolish to regard this as more than a suggestion; however, it would help to explain why there is no record of a landed Ó Pronntaigh or Brunty family in Monknewtown.

We have found that when Hugh left the Boyne he ran away to an area where the name of Brunty or Ó Pronntaigh was well known. Mount Pleasant lime-kilns were right at the heart of a hotbed of Irish poetry-making. Pádraig Ó Pronntaigh had lived there only a few years previously, where he had copied manuscripts and written religious and satiric verse. Positive proof that Pádraig was Hugh's father has eluded us, but he did originate in the mid-Ulster centre of the Brunty clan, as perhaps did Hugh. It must be thought possible that in escaping from Drogheda, Hugh knew where to run to. It is also odd that the Earl of Drogheda's main estates were at the two ends of Hugh's journey. However, the site of the lime-kilns had been McNeill territory since the late seventeenth century. It is possible that in Ballymascanlan Hugh made his first acquaintance with religion, at any rate since his early exile from mid-Ulster.

Hugh was not impressed by priests, but he learnt to read scripture in English, especially the New Testament. Possibly the Harshaws increased his Jacobin and republican tendencies, in which he seems to have been followed by Emily, to judge by her sympathetic treatment of rebels in Gondal. But he married a Catholic whose allegiance to any church other than the Roman was cosmetic. The family was not totally accepted by any religious denomination. Patrick inherited his father's ready tongue and sharply logical mode of argument; he was later to pass this to his daughters. Even in 1818 he protests against the English legal system. In 1793 he was appointed as a schoolmaster though only sixteen, and followed Hugh in being most popular with young people. This talent passed to Anne and possibly Branwell, but not Charlotte or Emily. But all the Brontës had a vital interest in education, just as much as in weaving stories.

Romantic indiscretion brought about the end of Patrick's school-teaching in Glascar, just like Branwell in Thorpe Green. His next brother was involved in another kind of romantic dream: revolution. He fled from Ballynahinch like a Gondal outlaw. Patrick soon left Ireland, but his brothers stayed behind. They eked out a living building roads, but remained eccentric, howling at the funeral of Walsh's son, fighting at fairs, pretending to be ghosts, and taunting the devil for fun. Hugh and James both came to England to see their brother who had 'got on', were well treated, and set on their road home, somewhat disgusted with fantastical Branwell and sharp-eyed Charlotte in her parlour, but with warm memories of Anne who wanted to come home. The Haworth Brontës went back to idealising respectable Irishmen like Tom Moore and the Duke of Wellington.

Charlotte had winced at these visits but told herself Jamie was respectable, a 'yeoman', not a roadmender. Ireland meant only bitterness to her. Emily did not see it that way. She liked to pretend she was 'Iernë', the lonely Irish girl, or Geraldine, the dark-haired princess of treachery and slaughter, straight from Celtic legend. She wished to be 'as God made' her. God had given her a manic temper and a gift of balladry, a sharp musical ear and the ability to shoot straight with a gun as though shooting Welsh guards. She felt like a bard, like Mac Labhraí the harper of the 'Connspoid', whose anglicised name would have been McClory. In particular, God had given her the hereditary art of oral story-telling, so that she put her story in an audible form, making it possible for us to *hear* 'Nelly', as she tells a tale one of whose many bases may have been the grasping uncle Welsh in Yorkshire dress.

Appendix: Irish Writers in South Ulster/North Leinster in the Eighteenth Century

It has been suggested that during the nineteenth century Drogheda was a centre of Irish literary tradition. During the previous century, when Hugh Brunty was growing up in the Boyne valley and near Mount Pleasant just north of Dundalk, there were many poets and scribes at work in this area. Even if *Pádraig Ó Pronntaigh* was not Hugh's father, even if there was no family connection between them, it seems probable that a story-teller with an Irish language background, such as I hope I have shown to be the most probable interpretation of Wright's account of Hugh, would have met and been party to the work of some of the men mentioned below.

Peadar Ó Duirnín was born about 1704 at Raskeagh, two or three miles north of Dundalk, and within a mile of Mount Pleasant. He taught at a school near Dundalk, where he had as patrons a family called *Colman*. They lived at Ballybarrack, and feature in the County Louth corn census. Another patron was *Arthur Brownlow* of Lurgan, County Down. At some point he also kept a school at Forkhill, five miles from Dundalk and two from his birthplace. Here he quarrelled with another poet, *Muiris Ó Gorman*. He died there in 1768. One of the best manuscripts of his poems was copied in 1792 for *Samuel Coulter*, an Irish scholar of Carnbeg, half a mile from Mount Pleasant. Among Ó Duirnín's poems are satires, love poems, vision poems, political and religious works. Two dramatic poems are set in Drogheda.

Muiris Ó Gorman, just mentioned, whose birthplace is unknown, was a teacher at Forkhill. He taught pupils from County Armagh and County Cavan, but was attacked by *Peadar Ó Duirnín* for his defective English. He was employed for a time by *Charles O'Connor* of Belanagare, where he copied Irish annals.

Appendix 153

Séamus Mac Cuarta, whose work was copied by Pádraig Ó Pronntaigh, was probably born at Kilcurly, three miles west of Dundalk and five from Mount Pleasant, at the end of the seventeenth century. He may have lived for a time at Kells, higher up the Boyne than Slane. In calling it 'Ceannanus *na ccros go droichiot Áth*' he shows that the name of Drogheda was not confined rigidly to the town, and that when Hugh Brunty's descendants described him as coming from Drogheda, they may quite possibly have meant the country beyond the town itself. Séamus says that eight of his family are buried near the Boyne. He writes a poem in praise of the men of Slane in their football match against the men of the River Nanny.

There were apparently two poets of the name *Pádraig Mac Alindon*. The name appears in several South Down townlands in the nineteenth century, but Pádraig the elder kept a school at Cnoc Chéin Mhic Chainte, Dundalk, for the reading and writing of Irish manuscripts. He had either a sister or daughter who was involved in a poetic contest with *Peadar Ó Duirnín*, for the tradition accepted women poets. The younger Mac Alindon was apparently a good poet and harper, but of eccentric habits. He seems to have spent much of his time in South Armagh, where we found several members of the Brunty clan on the Hearth Money rolls. Also from South Armagh, Creggan parish, was *Art Mac Cubhthaigh*, who wrote the funeral elegy for *Peadar Ó Duirnín*. He was born about 1715 and spent his life as a jobbing gardener. His poems were collected and published in 1916 by Henry Morris. He is buried at Creggan, having died about 1792. *Aodh (Hugh) Mac Gerraghty* was probably a farmer at Mount Sion, Dundalk, and wrote a burlesque of himself as 'high president' of Mount Sion, engaged in a boar hunt. *Peadar Ó Dálaigh* was a later poet who kept a school at Ardbreccan in the Boyne valley, about four miles from Navan. Two Newry scribes at the end of the eighteenth century were *Aodh Ó Néill* and *Pádraig O Héthir*.

Many of these scribes and poets had close links with Dundalk. They seem to have kept themselves in various ways involving manual labour as well as school-teaching. Much less attention has been given to their work than that of earlier generations of Irish poets and it is hard to find texts of their poems, let alone English translations. Some issues of the *County Louth Archæological and Historical Society Journal* do contain examples, with commentary. That they were highly skilled verbal technicians appears from a cursory reading, but any hope of detailed scholarly comparison of their work with that of the Brontë sisters must await the interest of someone with much more knowledge of Irish language and literature than I.

Notes

Where full publication details are not given here, they will be found in the Select Bibliography at the end of the book.

NOTES TO CHAPTER 1: INTRODUCTION

1. Letter from Mary Taylor to Mrs Gaskell, 28 January 1856, quoted in E. C. Gaskell, *The Life of Charlotte Brontë*, p. 65 (Everyman edn).
2. There is a good deal of variation in the way the Brontës wrote their name. The final syllable sometimes has an acute, sometimes a grave accent, sometimes a diæresis. See J. Horsfall Turner, *Brontëana*, p. 285.
3. W. Wright, *The Brontës in Ireland*. See early copies of the *Brontë Society Transactions* for Wright on the list of vice-presidents. But he merits no obituary in the issue of 1900.

NOTES TO CHAPTER 2: WILLIAM WRIGHT

1. G. E. Harrison, *The Clue to the Brontës*, p. 3; C. K. Shorter, *Charlotte Brontë and her Circle*, p. 137.
2. There is a gap in the records of the Belfast Royal Academical Institution from 1838 to 1859.
3. Letter from James Robertson recommending Wright, Glasgow University Library.
4. J. Ramsden, *The Brontë Homeland, or Misrepresentations Rectified*, pp. 142, 167.

NOTES TO CHAPTER 3: AN IRISH PRESBYTERIAN MILIEU

1. *McClure's Magazine*, vol. I (1893) p. 535.
2. Letter from John Brontë to William Wright, *The Bookman*, February 1897, p. 175.
3. Wright, *Brontës in Ireland*, pp. 6, 214, 218.
4. Ibid., p. 215.
5. Copy of Glascar Meeting-house register, at PRONI.
6. For Derrydrummuck Mill, see Ordnance Survey report, parish of Aghaderg, Royal Irish Academy.

7. According to a note supplied to me through Miss Muriel Greene, quoting the Revd Kirkpatrick of The Hill church.
8. Presbyterian Historical Society, *A History of Congregations in the Presbyterian Church of Ireland 1610–1892*, pp. 298–9.
9. Wright, *Brontës in Ireland*, p. 7.
10. Ibid., pp. 46–7.
11. *The Banbridge Chronicle*, 7 September 1918.
12. Facsimile in Wright, *Brontës in Ireland*, p. 269.
13. Wright's description (ibid., chs. II and XXVIII) is partly based on the eye-witness account of his wife.
14. *The Sketch*, vol. 17 (10 February 1897) p. 118.
15. *Notes & Queries*, 8th series, vol. VII (26 January 1895) p. 71.
16. *Brontë Society Transactions*, pt 8 (1898) pp. 6–7
17. *Notes & Queries*, vol. VII, p. 71.
18. For his baptism see Glascar Meeting-house register.
19. Wright, *Brontës in Ireland*, p. 49.
20. See R. Moore, *A Life of William Dobbin*; J. Y. McKee, *A History of the Descendants of David McKee of Annahilt;* J. Moorhead, *First and Second Anaghlone*.
21. Moorhead, ibid., p. 13.
22. Ibid., p. 21.

NOTES TO CHAPTER 4: THE BRONTË SENSATION

1. For the titles of the books referred to, see the Select Bibliography.
2. A. M. McKay, 'A Crop of Brontë Myths', *The Westminster Review*, vol. 144 (1895) pp. 424ff.
3. *The Bookman*, vol. 11 (February 1897) pp. 139ff.
4. Ramsden, *Brontë Homeland*, pp. 37, 60.
5. McKay, 'A Crop of Brontë Myths', pp. 120, 160; *Sketch*, vol. 17 (1897) p. 118; Turner, *Brontëana*, p. 292.
6. Obituary in *The Banbridge Chronicle*, 21 January 1891.
7. *The Sketch*, vol. 17 (March 1897) p. 288.
8. Obituary, *The Banbridge Chronicle*, 21 January 1891.
9. Wright, *Brontës in Ireland*, p. 157.
10. Ibid., p. 160.
11. *The Bookman*, vol. 11 (March 1897) p. 175.
12. A. M. McKay, *The Brontës: Fact and Fiction*, p. 142.
13. Ibid.
14. *The Bookman*, vol. 11 (December 1896) pp. 63ff.
15. McKay, *The Brontës: Fact and Fiction*, p. 142.
16. *The Bookman*, vol. 11 (March 1897) p. 65.
17. *The Sketch*, vol. 17 (March 1897) p. 288.
18. See, e.g., Barbara M. Kerr, 'Irish Seasonal Migration to Great Britain, 1800–1838', *Irish Historical Studies*, III (1943) pp. 365–80.
19. Letters from Wright to Rose Heslip, 22 and 23 August 1893, in the Brontë Parsonage Museum.
20. *The Sketch*, vol. 17 (February 1897) p. 118.

21. Ibid., vol. 17 (March 1897) p. 288.
22. *The Academy*, vol. 44 (1893) pp. 523, 550, 569, 589; vol. 45 (1894) pp. 15ff.

NOTES TO CHAPTER 5:   BRONTË ORIGINS

1. E. C. Gaskell, *The Life of Charlotte Brontë*, Ch. III.
2. Quoted, for example, in A. B. Hopkins, *The Father of the Brontës*, p. 3; MS in Christy Library, Manchester.
3. E. MacLysaght, *More Irish Families*, see under *Brontë*.
4. T. G. F. Paterson, *Harvest Home*, p. 170.
5. *Publications of the Royal Irish Society of Antiquaries*, vol. 22 (1892) p. 430.
6. G. Coffey, *New Grange*.
7. W. Y. Evans-Wentz, *The Fairy Faith in Celtic Countries*, pp. 34–7.
8. Ibid.
9. Estate map, National Library of Ireland, *per* Mr C. E. F. Trench; Earl of Sheffield's Irish rents, East Sussex Record Office.
10. Wright, *Brontës in Ireland*, p. 49.
11. *Banbridge Chronicle*, 21 January 1891.
12. E. C. Gaskell, *Letters*, p. 245.
13. The Ordnance Survey notes also mention this Scots flavour in Aghaderg.
14. Wright, *Brontës in Ireland*, pp. 46–7.
15. Ibid., p. 16.
16. Ibid., p. 17.
17. Ibid., p. 40.
18. Ibid., p. 40.
19. Ibid., p. 42.
20. Ibid., p. 45.
21. Ibid., p. 46.
22. *Folk Life*, vol. 2 (1963) pp. 36–7.
23. McKay, *The Brontës: Fact and Fiction*, pp. 121–2.
24. Wright, *Brontës in Ireland*, p. 49.

NOTES TO CHAPTER 6:   FROM THE BOYNE TO IMDEL

1. J. Cannon, *The Road to Haworth*, p. 26.
2. Liverpool Port Books, microfilm at Liverpool Public Library.
3. Wright, *Brontës in Ireland*, p. 17.
4. Townley Hall papers, National Library of Ireland, *per* C. E. F. Trench. Mr Noel Ross of Dundalk tells me that Anthony Walsh, or Welsh, was steward at Mellifont from at least 1714.
5. P. B. Eustace, *Abstract of Wills: Dublin Registry of Deeds*, vol. 1 (Dublin, 1956) p. 359.
6. *County Louth Archæological and Historical Society Journal*, vol. 1 (1945).
7. Wright, *Brontës in Ireland*, pp. 32 and 68, tells a slightly incoherent story of an agent's murder and suggests that Welsh was attacked and his property burnt at the same time. The murder of Michael Walsh was the subject of an Irish House of Lords appeal as late as 1767 (information *per* Mr C. E. F. Trench).

8. S. Lewis, *Topographical Dictionary of Ireland* (London, 1837).
9. Hyde, *Literary History of Ireland*, p. 628.
10. Ramsden, *Brontë Homeland*, p. 44.
11. H. Morris, in *County Louth Archæological and Historical Society Journal*, vol. 3 (1947) p. 189, quoting Stuart's *History of Armagh*, pp. 266–7. He prints the complete poem in Irish. In a later (1759) MS at the British Library (Egerton 172), Pádraig Ó Pronntaigh apparently introduces the poem with the words 'Air teacht don phrionfháidh agus dá dhearbhráithre a chomhnuidhe go Baile Ui Sganláin'. The word *teacht* means 'coming' 'arrival', and thus seems to imply that Pádraig himself lived there at the time.
12. His actual word is 'ancestor' of Charlotte (Hyde, *Literary History of Ireland*, p. 258).
13. Wright, *Brontës in Ireland*, p. 16.
14. In an article on Omeath, *County Louth Archæological and Historical Society Journal*, vol. 3 (1947) p. 218.
15. S. Ó Casaide, *The Irish Language in Belfast and County Down, AD 1601–1850*, p. 26.
16. An eighteenth-century corn census of County Louth in *County Louth Archæological and Historical Society Journal*, vol. 2 (1945) p. 286.
17. O'Donovan's original letters are at the Royal Irish Academy; a printed version of those letters relating to County Down, by Browne & Nolan (Dublin, n.d.), is in the Linenhall Library at Belfast.
18. Wright, *Brontës in Ireland*, p. 151.
19. C. O'Byrne, *The Gælic Source of the Brontë Genius*, pp. 29ff.
20. Ó Casaide, *The Irish Language*, p. 56.
21. There are many versions of the Táin Bó. See Hyde, *Literary History of Ireland*, Ch. XXVI.
22. Wright, *Brontës in Ireland*, p. 48. For the style and repertoire of a seanchaí, see J. H. Delargy, 'The Gælic Storyteller', *Proceedings of the British Academy* (1945), the Sir John Rhys Memorial Lecture.
23. Wright, *Brontës in Ireland*, p. 171.
24. Ibid., p. 133.
25. Ibid., p. 130.
26. Ibid., p. 132.
27. Egerton 172, as described in R. Flower, *A Catalogue of the Irish Manuscripts in the British Museum*, vol. III (1926) p. 119.
28. Wright, *Brontës in Ireland*, p. 96.
29. J. D. Cowan, *Donaghmore: Past and Present*, pp. 319ff.
30. Wright, *Brontës in Ireland*, pp. 231–5.
31. *Clergy Succession Lists, Church of Ireland* (Magherally) (Belfast, n.d.) p. 206.

NOTES TO CHAPTER 7: BIRTH AND CHILDHOOD OF PATRICK BRONTË

1. Gaskell, *Life of Charlotte Brontë*, ch. III.
2. Shorter, *Charlotte Brontë and her Circle*, p. 28.

3. P. Bentley, *The Brontës and their World*, p. 3.
4. Horsfall Turner, *Brontëana*, p. 279.
5. Wright, *Brontës in Ireland*, p. 109.
6. Lock and Dixon, *Man of Sorrow*, p. 21.
7. Ramsden, *Brontë Homeland*, p. 41; O'Byrne, *The Gælic Source*, p. 24.
8. Ellen Nussey in *Scribner's Magazine*, May 1871.
9. Wright, *Brontës in Ireland*, pp. 114ff.
10. Ibid., pp. 131–2.
11. Ramsden, *Brontë Homeland*, p. 39.
12. *Banbridge Chronicle*, 7 September 1918.
13. Horsfall Turner, *Brontëana*, p. 275.
14. *Banbridge Chronicle*, 7 September 1918.
15. Wright, *Brontës in Ireland*, p. 228.
16. Ibid., p. 245.
17. S. Pender (ed.), *A Census of Ireland, c. 1659* (Dublin, 1939).
18. Perhaps from a note in McKay, *The Brontës: Fact and Fiction* in which he claims (p. 121) that Maggie Shannon had told him her grandfather Welsh was 'named after a clergyman' in their neighbourhood.
19. Horsfall Turner, *Brontëana*, pp. 290, 294.
20. Details of the dates of baptism of the Brontë brothers and sisters are from Wright, *Brontës in Ireland*, pp. 156–162, and Cannon, *Road to Haworth*, p. 71, supported by a Brontë genealogy at the Brontë Parsonage Museum.
21. Horsfall Turner, *Brontëana*, p. 292.

NOTES TO CHAPTER 8: THE YOUNG PATRICK

1. 'Statistical Remarks on Aghaderg Parish', OS Box 23 (Down) II Aghaderg, p. 9.
2. Information from the late Dr W. Haughton Crowe, Rostrevor, County Down.
3. Paterson, *Harvest Home*, p. 171, quoting *Belfast Newsletter*, 23 February 1937.
4. That Patrick was an unorthodox teacher appears clearly from Wright, *Brontës in Ireland*, ch. XXV, and may be underestimated in our assumptions concerning the children's upbringing at Haworth.
5. Harrison, *Clue to the Brontës*, p. 18; Cannon, *Road to Haworth*, pp. 82ff.; 'Application for Aid Towards Teacher's Salary at Glascar School' (PRONI EDI 16).
6. Ramsden, *Brontë Homeland*, pp. 38–9.
7. Wright, *Brontës in Ireland*, p. 251.
8. K. Meyer, in *Otia Merseiana*, vol. I (London, 1899).
9. Hyde, *Literary History of Ireland*, p. 200.
10. *Wildfell Hall*, ch. 49.
11. Wright, *Brontës in Ireland*, p. 250.
12. A list given in *The Bookman*, vol. II (February 1897) p. 139, mentions: an arithmetic book with signatures 'Patrick Prunty', bought in 1795; a New Testament (Oxford University Press, 1728), with 'Allie Brontë' written inside the back cover; Hugh Brontë's geography book with 'Hugh Bronte: his book

in the year 1803'. There is also at the Brontë Parsonage Museum a title-page, of a Bible with various signatures 'Brunty' or 'Bronte', part erased. See also Horsfall Turner, *Brontëana*, p. 284.
13. On page 256 he clearly suggests that the Revd John Rogers, appointed in 1798, was responsible for the dismissal, but lower down this page he suggests that the years 1797 and 1798 were miserable as Patrick found himself 'without employment'.
14. Wright, *Brontës in Ireland*, p. 243, quoting verbatim from a letter of W. J. McCracken.
15. Ibid., pp. 256–8.
16. Ramsden, *Brontë Homeland*, pp. 143–7.
17. Wright, *Brontës in Ireland*, pp. 256–8.
18. R. Barron, *Memoir of the Revd William Rogers*, pp. 4–5.
19. Derrydrummuck Mill: OS Box 23 Aghaderg, table of mills.
20. Information from the Revd W. Bailie, Kilmore, County Down.
21. Letter from Wright to Rose Heslip, 22 August 1893, at the Brontë Parsonage Museum.
22. Wright, *Brontës in Ireland*, esp. pp. 163ff.
23. E. A. Chadwick, *In the Footsteps of the Brontës*, pp. 74ff.
24. Paterson, *Harvest Home*, p. 91.
25. Wright, *Brontës in Ireland*, p. 167.
26. Ramsden, *Brontë Homeland*, pp. 67–8.
27. E. M. Clarke, *Round about Rathfriland*, p. 23.
28. Ibid., p. 46.
29. Harrison, *Clue to the Brontës*, pp. 11, 13.
30. Lock and Dixon, *Man of Sorrow*, p. 21.
31. *Notes and Queries*, 8th Series, vol. 7, 1895, p. 71.

NOTES TO CHAPTER 9: BRONTËS IN IRELAND

1. Information from the Revd Edward Simpson, March 1982.
2. Letter from Patrick Brontë to William Campbell, 12 November 1808, in Princeton University Library.
3. Lock and Dixon, *Man of Sorrow*, p. 334.
4. For example in Crowe, *Brontës of Ballynaskeagh*, p. 180.
5. Ibid.
6. Horsfall Turner, *Brontëana*, p. 288.
7. *The Bookman*, vol. 11 (February 1897) p. 175.
8. Horsfall Turner, *Brontëana*, p. 288.
9. *The Bookman*, vol. 11 (February 1897) p. 175.
10. Griffith's *Parish Valuation of Ireland*, Aghaderg parish (1864) pp. 54–5.

NOTES TO CHAPTER 10: WEIRD IRISH STORIES

1. Wright, *Brontës in Ireland*, p. 134.
2. A. M. F. Robinson, *Emily Brontë*, pp. 18, 27, 50–1. See also p. 160, where she specifically alludes to 'grisly Irish horrors, tales of 1798 . . .'.

3. Reprinted in *Brontë Society Transactions*, II, Pt X (1900) pp. 58–83.
4. T. Wemyss Reid, *Charlotte Brontë: A Monograph* (London, 1877) pp. 215–16.
5. Turner, *Brontëana*, p. 300.
6. *The Sketch*, vol. 17 (20 February 1897) p. 118.
7. *The Bookman*, vol. 11 (December 1896) p. 65.
8. Ramsden, *Brontë Homeland*, p. 161.
9. Ibid., pp. 161–2.
10. *The Bookman*, vol. 11 (December 1896). See also McKay, *The Brontës: Fact and Fiction*, p. 160.
11. Lock and Dixon, *Man of Sorrow*, p. 86.
12. Wright, *Brontës in Ireland*, p. 287.
13. Ibid., p. 291.
14. Ibid., p. 285.
15. Ibid., pp. 182–4; *The Sketch*, vol. 17 (February 1897) pp. 118.

NOTES TO CHAPTER 11: THE IRISH WRITING OF PATRICK BRONTË

1. Wright, *Brontës in Ireland*, pp. 249–50.
2. J. Erskine Stuart, *The Brontë Country*, p. 33.
3. Lock and Dixon, *Man of Sorrow*, p. 259.
4. W. G. Wood-Martin, *Traces of the Elder Faiths of Ireland*, vol. I, p. 311.
5. Ibid., vol. I, p. 313; vol. II, p. 394.
6. W. Scruton, *Thornton and the Brontës*, p. 59.
7. Ibid., pp. 66–7.
8. W. Gérin, *Branwell Brontë*, p. 5.

NOTES TO CHAPTER 12: 'WUTHERING HEIGHTS'

1. M. Allott, *The Brontës: The Critical Heritage*, p. 231.
2. D. du Maurier, *The Infernal World of Branwell Brontë*, pp. 44–5.
3. W. Gérin, *Emily Brontë*, p. 226.
4. Letter from Patrick Brontë to Mr Marriner, 10 November 1824; Gérin, *Emily Brontë*, p. 7.
5. *Wuthering Heights*, ch. 12.
6. Paterson, *Harvest Home*, p. 208.
7. Wood-Martin, *Traces of the Elder Faiths of Ireland*, vol. II, p. 296.
8. Wright, *Brontës in Ireland*, p. 47.
9. J. Simpson, 'The Function of Folklore in *Jane Eyre* and *Wuthering Heights*', *Folklore*, vol. 85 (1974) pp. 47ff.
10. J. F. Goodrich, 'A New Heaven and a New Earth', in A. Smith (ed.), *The Art of Emily Brontë*, p. 172.
11. F. J. Child, *The English and Scottish Popular Ballads* (New York, 1882) vol. II, pp. 63ff, 199ff. The collection does not exclude Irish ballads, but there are comparatively few of them.
12. Ibid., p. 77.

13. H. Shields, 'Old British Ballads in Ireland', *Folklife*, vol. 10 (1972) pp. 68ff.
14. J. H. Delargey, 'The Gælic Storyteller', *Proceedings of the British Academy* (1945).
15. Wright, *Brontës in Ireland*, p. 8.

NOTES TO CHAPTER 13:   LYRIC POEMS AND REBELLION IN GONDAL

1. O'Byrne, *The Gælic Source of the Brontë Genius*, pp. 29ff.
2. Ibid., p. 33.
3. For example, in J. Reeves, *The Idiom of the People* (London, 1958) p. 70.
4. C. W. Hatfield (ed.), *The Complete Poems of Emily Jane Brontë* (New York, 1941) p. 90.
5. 'Ula' is the name of a southern island in Emily's poems (ibid., nos 141 and 166).
6. Ibid., nos 46 and 177. 'Iernë' is used as a name for Ireland in Strabo's Geography. Moore (*History of Ireland*, vol. I, p. 7) draws attention to what he considers the first historical record of the 'two chief British islands ... under their old Celtic names of Albion and Iernë' in the *de Mundo* attributed to Aristotle.
7. It may seem rash to assert the self-identification here. It would need considerable space to argue the point; I have done so briefly in my *Brontë Facts and Brontë Problems*, written with Tom Winnifrith (London, 1983), see esp. ch. 5.
8. Wright, *Brontës in Ireland*, p. 150.
9. *McComb's Guide to Belfast*, pp. 121ff.
10. E. Chitham, *The Poems of Anne Brontë* (London, 1979) p. 121.
11. Hatfield, *Complete Poems of Emily Brontë*, no. 192.
12. Letter from Patrick Brontë to Hugh Brontë, 2 December 1858, most recently reprinted in W. H. Crowe, *The Brontës of Ballynaskeagh*, p. 180.
13. *McComb's Guide to Belfast*, p. 136.

NOTES TO CHAPTER 14:   CHARLOTTE'S IRISH ACCENT

1. Wright, *Brontës in Ireland*, pp. 10–13, 268ff.
2. Ibid., p. 274.
3. See C. Brontë, *Shirley*, ed. H. Rosengarten and M. Smith (London, 1979) p. 724 and notes, pp. 743, 786.
4. Ibid., pp. 11–14.
5. Ibid., p. 17.
6. See Gérin, *Charlotte Brontë*, pp. 514ff.

Select Bibliography

1 BOOKS REFERRING TO THE BRONTËS' IRISH ANCESTRY OR TO THE BRONTËS AS WRITERS

Allot, M. (ed.), *The Brontës: The Critical Heritage* (London, 1974).
Bentley, P., *The Brontës and their World* (London, 1969).
Cannon, J., *The Road to Haworth* (London, 1979).
Chadwick, E. A., *In the Footsteps of the Brontës* (London, 1914).
Crowe, W. H., *The Brontës of Ballynaskeagh* (Dundalk, 1978).
du Maurier, D., *The Infernal World of Branwell Brontë* (London, 1972).
Gaskell, E. C., *Letters*, ed. J. A. V. Chappell and A. Pollard (Manchester, 1966).
Gaskell, E. C., *The Life of Charlotte Brontë* (London, 1857).
Gérin, W., *Branwell Brontë* (London, 1961).
Gérin, W., *Charlotte Brontë* (London, 1967).
Gérin, W., *Emily Brontë* (London, 1971).
Harrison, G. E., *The Clue to the Brontës* (London, 1948).
Hatfield, C. W., *The Complete Poems of Emily Jane Brontë* (Columbia, 1941).
Hopkins, A. B., *The Father of the Brontës* (Baltimore, 1958).
Lock, J. and Dixon, W. T., *A Man of Sorrow* (London, 1965).
McKay, A. M., *The Brontës: Fact and Fiction* (London, 1897).
O'Byrne, C., *The Gælic Source of the Brontë Genius* (Edinburgh, 1933).
Ramsden, J., *The Brontë Homeland, or Misrepresentations Rectified* (London, 1897).
Robinson, A. M. F., *Emily Brontë* (London, 1883).
Scruton, W., *Thornton and the Brontës* (Bradford, 1898).
Shorter, C. K., *Charlotte Brontë and her Circle* (London, 1896).
Smith, A., *The Art of Emily Brontë* (London, 1976).
Stuart, J. Erskine, *The Brontë Country* (London, 1888).
Turner, J. Horsfall, *Brontëana* (Bingley, 1898).
Wright, W., *The Brontës in Ireland* (New York, 1893).

2 PRINTED BOOKS REFERRING TO IRELAND ETC.

Allen, R., *The Presbyterian College, Belfast 1853–1953* (Belfast, 1954).
Barron, R., *Memoir of the Revd William Rogers* (Belfast, 1898).
Binns, J., *The Miseries and Beauties of Ireland* (London, 1837).
Clarke, E. M., *City Set on a Hill* (Rathfriland, 1979).
Clarke, E. M., *Round about Rathfriland* (Rathfriland, 1981).

Clergy Succession Lists, Church of Ireland (Belfast, n.d.).
Coffey, G., *New Grange* (London, 1912).
Cowan, J. D., *Donaghmore: Past and Present* (London, 1914).
Evans-Wentz, W. Y., *The Fairy Faith in Celtic Countries* (Oxford, 1911).
Flower, R., *Catalogue of the Irish Manuscripts in the British Museum*, vol. III (London, 1926).
Hyde, D., *A Literary History of Ireland* (London, 1899).
Irish Manuscripts Commission, *'Census' of Ireland, 1659* (Dublin, 1939).
McComb's Guide to Belfast (Belfast, 1861).
McKee, J. Y., *A History of the Descendants of David McKee of Annahilt* (Philadelphia, 1892).
MacLysaght, E., *More Irish Families* (Dublin, 1960).
Moore, R., *A Life of William Dobbin* (Belfast, n.d.).
Moorhead, J., *First and Second Anaghlone* (Belfast, n.d.).
Ó Casaide, S., *The Irish Language in Belfast and County Down, AD 1601–1850* (Dublin, 1930).
Paterson, T. G. F., *Harvest Home* (Armagh, 1975).
Presbyterian Historical Society, *A History of Congregations in the Presbyterian Church of Ireland, 1610–1982* (Belfast, 1982).
Wood-Martin, W. G., *Traces of the Elder Faiths of Ireland*, 2 vols (London, 1902).
(title-page missing), *History of First Ballyeaston Church* (n.d.).

Index

Aengus, King, 38, 52
Aghaderg (Ahaderg), 12, 17, 19, 26, 33, 56, 64, 73, 78, 97
Annaclone (Anaclone, etc.), 63, 73, 78
Arabian storytellers, 13
Armagh, County, 27, 139
Aykroyd, Tabitha, 111, 125

Ballad tradition, 128–31
Ballymascanlan, 51–3, 55–7, 60, 62
Ballynahinch, 20, 27–8, 57, 68, 74, 103, 137–40, 150
Ballynaskeagh, 4, 9, 10, 14–15, 17–19, 21–2, 28, 30–1, 42, 56, 64, 66–7, 76–7, 82, 85–6, 90, 93, 95–7, 104, 111, 120, 128, 144
Banbridge, 5, 17, 26, 72, 77, 91
Banim, John, 123
Barber, Samuel, 9, 70, 73
Belfast, 7, 19
Bentley, Phyllis, 5
Better house, the, 66
Boyne farmhouse, 36, 42, 46–7, 49–52, 74, 132
Boyne river, 4, 34, 36–9, 42–4, 52–3
British and Foreign Bible Society, 7, 17
Brontë, *see also* Brunty
Brontë, Alice, 17, 24–6, 43, 53, 62, 66–7, 69, 92, 97, 104, 107–8
Brontë, Anne, 70, 78–9, 83, 100, 107, 111–12, 114, 131, 134–5, 138, 150
Brontë, Charlotte, 1–2, 7, 24, 27–8, 31–4, 43, 67, 78, 86, 89, 93, 104–8, 121–2, 142–8, 150
Brontë, Elizabeth, 79, 87
Brontë, Emily Jane, 1, 3, 7, 19, 33,
    39, 50, 76, 78, 93, 97, 101–2, 104, 108, 119, 121, 123–35, 138–40, 145, 150–1
personae of, 33, 136–7, 151
Brontë family
    anti-clerical tradition, 68
    diet, 66–7
    educational views, 78–9
    fear of fire, 67
    folk artistry, 67, 86
    oral language, 68–9
    practical jokes, 29, 75, 95–6
    religion, 18–19, 34
    revolutionary politics, 68
    swearing, 68
    works of, *see* Brontë works
Brontë, Hugh, 14–16, 24, 27, 29, 31, 75, 94–7, 103, 109–11, 139, 144, 148
    visits to England, 29–30, 105–7, 110–11
Brontë, James, 24–5, 27, 29–30, 39, 75, 97, 99, 103, 105
    visits to England, 29–31, 105, 107–8, 150
Brontë, Jane, 24, 76, 114
Brontë, John, 10, 25–8, 74–5, 94
Brontë kiln (Patrick's birthplace), 19, 47, 56, 64–5, 82, 96, 99
Brontë, Maria, 70, 79, 87, 122
Brontë, Mary, 24, 27, 76, 94
Brontë, Patrick, 1–2, 6, 9, 14–15, 21, 24–31, 33–4, 42–3, 47, 49, 57, 64–74, 76–9, 81, 82, 84, 86, 89, 92–5, 97, 100–8, 113–21, 128, 131, 135, 137, 140, 146, 148–9
Brontë, Patrick Branwell, 1, 3–4, 76, 90, 100, 108–9, 111–12, 124–5, 140–1, 150

165

Brontë, Rose, 24, 76
Brontë, Sarah, 24–5, 30, 76, 94, 105
Brontë Society in the 1890s, 2, 32
Brontë, Welsh (Walsh), 16, 24–5, 28, 30–1, 73, 75, 95, 97, 99, 106
Brontë, William, 24–7, 74, 87, 97, 103, 137, 139
Brontë works
  An Adventure in Ireland, 142–3
  Cottage in the Wood, The, 114
  Cottage Poems, 80, 113–14
  Gondal poems and saga, 27, 33, 58, 68, 97, 124, 137–40, 150
  Jane Eyre, 9, 14–16, 21, 29, 109–11, 122, 127, 133, 142–4, 149
  lyric poems, 134–8
  Maid of Killarney, The, 60, 71, 114–18, 122, 126, 128, 137
  'rough' poems of Patrick, 80
  Rural Minstrel, The, 114–15
  Search after Happiness, The, 143
  Shirley, 142, 146–8
  Signs of the Times, 121
  Tenant of Wildfell Hall, The, 79, 83, 118, 122, 141
  Treatise on Baptism, 122
  Wuthering Heights, 33, 57, 69, 95, 101–2, 123–33, 148–9
Brown, Martha, 103
Brownlow, Arthur, 152
Brugh na Boinne, 37
Brunty, Alice (Eilís, Eleanor), *see* McClory
Brunty, Hugh (Patrick's father), 4, 9, 11–13, 17, 19–25, 28, 29, 32, 33, 36–7, 38–9, 41–4, 46, 47, 49–50, 55, 56, 58–61, 64, 65, 67–9, 71, 74, 79–80, 82, 85, 97, 119, 133, 143, 145
Brunty, 'Mary' (Hugh's aunt), 28, 31, 39, 50–2, 68
Brunty, 'Mary' (Hugh's sister or cousin), 28
Brunty name, origin of, *see* Pronty
Burns, Joseph, 62, 99, 132
Burns, Robert, 67, 87

Calvinism, 86
Cambridge, 1, 7, 34, 91, 100, 140

Campbell, Elizabeth, 75, 95
Cannon, John, 5, 17
Castlewellan, 42, 56, 90
Catholic religion, 55, 60, 62, 64–7, 70–1, 104, 118
Ceilidh in the glen, 10, 86–7, 89
Celtic oral tradition, 13, 58–9, 67, 100, 126, 128, 131
Church of Ireland, 70–3
Coulter, Samuel, 152
Crewbane, 41
Crowe, W. Haughton, 5, 159

Davidson, Samuel, 7
Derrydrummuck, 11, 85
Dewsbury, Yorks, 115
Donaghmore (Donoughmore), 56, 60–1, 131
Donald, Robert, 71
Down, County, 2, 21, 24, 26, 56, 131, 139
Dowth, 52
Drogheda, 4, 24–5, 28–9, 31, 34, 42, 46, 48–50, 52, 149–50, 152
Drumballyroney, 17, 56, 64–6, 73–4, 78, 89–90, 92
Drumballyroney school, 83
Drumgooland, 64, 90, 91
Dundalk, 4, 19, 47–8, 51, 55, 57, 152–3

Edgar, John, 21
Evangelicalism, 73, 87

Faughart (Farghart), 53
Finard (Finnards), 6, 12
Flanigan, Alex, 77
Fletcher family, 85
Foundlings in Ireland, 49
Frazer, an old man of Imdel, 19, 71

Gallagher, 39, 41, 50, 52
Gaskell, Mrs E. C., 1, 3, 9, 33–4, 43, 64, 66, 77, 87, 89, 101, 131, 143
Gérin, Winifred, 5, 125
Glascar, 9, 11, 17, 19, 21, 53, 56, 60, 66, 70–5, 77, 79–84, 90, 113, 121, 150

Index

Glascar meeting house register, 77, 85
Glascar school, 79–80
Glasgow University, 7
Greek myth and legend, 13, 52

Harrison, Elsie, 6, 11, 71–3, 79
Harshaw family, 56, 60–2, 71, 90
Hartshead, Yorks, 93, 107, 121, 147
Haworth, 26–9, 32, 57, 66, 68–9, 76, 96–7, 108, 110–12, 114, 136, 140
Heathcliff, 4, 38, 50, 124–5, 132–3
Heslip, Rose, 16–7, 24–5, 28–30, 68, 74, 85, 96, 105–9
Hilltown, 28–9, 47, 78
Horn signal, 88
Horsfall Turner, J., 3, 20, 23, 30, 32, 65, 71, 75–6, 92, 95–6, 104–5

Imdel (Emdale), 35, 49, 61, 64–5, 67, 114
Irish character, 120, 143, 148
Irish (English) language, 43, 56
Irish folk tradition, 13, 49, 53, 57, 59, 68, 82, 88–9, 104, 126–8, 135–6
Irish funeral customs, 116–18
Irish (Gaelic) language, 26, 46, 55–7
Irish literature, 13, 38, 53, 55, 57–9, 68–9, 81–3, 104, 115, 128, 134, 152–4

Keeper's antecedents, 119
Killarney, 34, 43, 47
Knowth, 4, 52

Lang, Andrew, 23, 31
Lett, Revd Henry, 17
Lindsay, John, 78
Lisnacreevy, 66, 76, 97
Liverpool, 1, 4, 16, 49, 112, 124–6, 132
Long bullets, 88
Loughbrickland, 72–3
Loughorne, 9, 61
Louth, County, 52, 57–8
Lusk, Revd J. B., 17–19, 25, 70–1, 85, 92

Mac Alindon, Pádraig, 153
McAlister family, 85
McAlister, John, 11
McAlister, Robert, 80, 85
McAlister, Samuel, 11, 13, 21, 80
McAlister, Revd William, 11–14, 20–1, 25, 44, 53, 58, 67, 69, 78, 85–9, 92
McArdle, Dean, of Aghaderg, 56
McClory, Alice (Eilís, Eleanor), 4, 12, 19, 31, 56, 60–2, 71
McClory family, 62, 66, 71, 97, 99
McClory, Paddy (servant), 19
McClory, Paddy (uncle), 56, 62, 97
McCormick, Revd William, 63
McCracken, Revd William John, 19, 21, 42–3, 69, 79–80, 83
Mac Cuarta, Séamus, 153
Mac Cubhthaigh, Art, 153
McFaddon, Henry, 69, 80
Mac Gerraghty, Hugh, 153
McKay, Angus, 3, 23–4, 29–30, 32, 34, 110–11
McKee, Annie, 15–16, 109–10, 145
McKee, Revd David, 14–16, 19–22, 31, 44, 69, 73, 78, 80, 99, 109–12, 144–6
MacLysaght, Edward, 35
McMahon, Bernard, Archbishop of Armagh, 55
McNeill family of Ballymascanlan, 55
Magherally, 4, 62–3
Magpie's blood as a charm, 31
Mellifont, 52–3
Merriman, Brian, 81, 83
Methodism, 70, 73
Monknewtown, 36–7, 39, 51, 149
Moore, Revd Alexander, 84
Moore, Thomas, 42, 137, 140
Mount Pleasant lime-kilns, 17, 19, 51, 53, 55–7, 149
Mourne mountains, 5

Neagh, Lough, 48, 107
Nesbit, Caleb, 10–11
Nesbit, Margaret, 10–11
Netterville family, 52
New Grange, 37–8, 41–2, 47, 52

Newry, 5, 27
Nicholls, Revd Arthur Bell, 95, 122, 148
Norton, Hugh, 19–20
Nussey, Ellen, 67, 69, 93, 96, 100, 102–3, 105, 108, 123, 125

O'Byrne, Cathal, 57
O'Connor, Charles, 152
Ó Dálaigh, Peadar, 153
O'Donovan, John, ix, 56
Ó Duirnín, Peadar, 152
Ó Gorman, Muiris, 152
Ó Héthir, Pádraig, 153
Ó Néill, Aodh, 153
Ó Pronntaigh, Pádraig, 35, 51, 53, 55–6, 58–9, 114, 131, 149, 152
O'Pronty surname, *see* Pronty

Palmer, Professor E. H., 7
Parish Valuation of Ireland, 34, 37, 41, 62, 85, 97
Paterson, T. G. F., 35, 88, 127
Penistone Crag, 126
Peters, Margot, 5
Postbox in tree, 61
Presbyterianism, 5, 7–8, 10, 12, 23, 55–6, 60, 62, 64, 70, 72, 77–8, 84, 89–90
Pronty surname, origins, 34–6, 48, 55, 59–60
Prunty, Frank, ferryman, 24

Quarterly, The, 16, 110–11
Queen's College, Belfast, 7

Radcliffe's mill, 96
Ramsden, J., 8, 21, 23–4, 30, 32, 34, 53, 69, 71, 80, 84, 106
Rathfriland, 6, 9, 35, 42, 47, 56, 63, 72–3, 77, 82, 95
Reid, T. Wemyss, 102, 123
Reid, W. Mayne, 20
Robertson, James, 7–8

Robinson, A. M. F., 17, 101, 104, 123
Rogers, Revd John, 84
Rosnaree, 36, 38, 39
Ryans, Finard, 12

Scots accent in County Down, 26, 43
Scots element in Ulster, 26, 42, 56, 72, 78
Scots Gaelic, 55
Shannon, Maggie, 17, 25, 28–9, 73–4, 96, 105–6
Shields, Hugh, 131
Shorter, Clement, 3, 6, 23, 32
Slane, 39
Synod of Ulster, 55

Táin Bó Cuailgne, 57
Tara, Kings of, 38, 42
Taylor, Mary, 1, 43, 100
'Tenant Right' in Ulster, 23
Tighe, Thomas, 9, 65, 71, 73, 89–91
Tithe Applotment (Ireland), 97
Todd brothers, 19, 99
Tumuli at Brugh na Boinne, 38, 41–2

Victoria, Queen, 107

Walsh family of Brugh na Boinne, 41–2, 51
Walsh, widow, 52
Warrenpoint, 14, 61, 112
'Welsh', the foundling, 16, 28, 30, 44, 46, 49–50, 71, 74–5, 132–3, 145, 151
    death of, 31
Wesley, John, 72–3
Wilson, Elizabeth, 19, 42, 69, 79, 83
Wright, Revd William, 2–32, 34, 36–7, 41, 43–4, 46–7, 49–50, 53, 60–1, 64–7, 69, 73, 80, 83–4, 93–7, 99–100, 105–12, 119, 121, 132